SAFEKEEPING

A Writer's Guided Journal for Launching a Book with Love

CHELENE KNIGHT

FOREWORD BY IVAN COYOTE

AMBROSIA

Published in Canada and the usa in 2025 by House of Anansi Press Inc.
houseofanansi.com

House of Anansi Press is committed to protecting our natural environment. This book is made of material from well-managed FSC®-certified forests, recycled materials, and other controlled sources.

House of Anansi Press is a Global Certified Accessible™ (GCA by Benetech) publisher. The ebook version of this book meets stringent accessibility standards and is available to readers with print disabilities.

29 28 27 26 25   1 2 3 4 5

Library and Archives Canada Cataloguing in Publication

Title: Safekeeping : a writer's guided journal for launching a book with love / Chelene Knight ; foreword by Ivan Coyote.

Names: Knight, Chelene, 1981- author | Coyote, Ivan, 1969- writer of foreword

Identifiers: Canadiana (print) 20240461142 | Canadiana (ebook) 20240461215 | ISBN 9781487013073 (softcover) | ISBN 9781487013080 (EPUB)

Subjects: LCSH: Authorship—Handbooks, manuals, etc. | LCSH: Authorship—Vocational guidance. | LCGFT: Handbooks and manuals. | LCGFT: Instructional and educational works.

Classification: LCC PN153 .K65 2025 | DDC 808.02—dc23

Book design: Alysia Shewchuk

House of Anansi Press is grateful for the privilege to work on and create from the Traditional Territory of many Nations, including the Anishinabeg, the Wendat, and the Haudenosaunee, as well as the Treaty Lands of the Mississaugas of the Credit.

Canada Council for the Arts | Conseil des Arts du Canada

ONTARIO ARTS COUNCIL
CONSEIL DES ARTS DE L'ONTARIO
an Ontario government agency
un organisme du gouvernement de l'Ontario

With the participation of the Government of Canada
Avec la participation du gouvernement du Canada | Canada

We acknowledge for their financial support of our publishing program the Canada Council for the Arts, the Ontario Arts Council, and the Government of Canada.

Printed and bound in Canada

FSC
www.fsc.org
MIX
Paper | Supporting responsible forestry
FSC® C103567

ADVANCE PRAISE FOR *SAFEKEEPING*

"Chelene Knight has created something that every writer needs, no matter where they are on their path—peace of mind. It is perhaps the most difficult of things to maintain and the most necessary. As writers, we are blessed/cursed with a vivid imagination that can aid and abet our inner critic. Knight has conjured a way to harness that power for good and give writers exactly the space and encouragement needed in order to be great and, more importantly, to thrive in what can be the harrowing experience of laying your soul bare on the page. This guided journal is a sharp tool and a precious gift for all writers." —CHERIE DIMALINE, author of *VenCo*

"Writing and publishing is a long journey, but it doesn't have to be painful. In *Safekeeping*, Chelene Knight identifies the core emotional and practical experiences in the creative writing process and helps us assemble a survival kit. Writers at every level of experience will benefit from these exercises. Knight guides writers through the literary landscape and helps us see that we have the power and the talent to put down those words, to finish that draft, to see that story come to life. This book is a gift!" —CARLEIGH BAKER, author of *Last Woman*

"*Safekeeping* is a gift worth many times its weight in gold for anyone aspiring to make creative writing part of their career. Current, comprehensive, and full of care, it is both a guided journal and a resource library with pertinent and candid storytelling weaving it all together." —KAI THOMAS, author of *In the Upper Country*

"Move over, *The Artist's Way*! This is the book we've been waiting for: *Safekeeping* provides the key to unlock our creativity, regardless of our artistic dreams. Chelene Knight walks us through our fears with great care, offering gentle reminders of our potential. Each and every page guides us to build our confidence as artists, opening up spaces for more creative flow and reminding us of our passions and promise. If you've ever felt blocked, or just don't know where to start as a creative: this is the book to help you begin your journey." —MINELLE MAHTANI, author of *May It Have a Happy Ending*

"There are many books that presume to tell you how to write, but Chelene Knight has written the first book I've seen about managing the complexities of life as a writer. Whether she's exploring expectations, ambitions, or time management, there is a structured approach to *Safekeeping* that can offer support for writers at any phase of their career." —PATRICK TARR, screenwriter and author of *The Guest Children*

"Chelene's profound new journal has wiped away the mystery of book writing. This book is a must-read for anyone looking to bring their writing to life." —CORY ALLEN, author of *Brave New You*

CONTENTS

PART 2: PUBLISHING

PART 3: AFTER PUBLISHING

FOREWORD

The Same Things So Much Differently

I came to the page via the stage, which I know is not the usual how-to-get-published story. I started telling my weird little queer stories on mini stages in East Vancouver in the early '90s: A ragged bunch of poets, storytellers, songwriters, and a one-man jug band created and crafted and experimented and still somehow got up on time to get to our day jobs.

And then writer, painter, and Commercial Drive lesbian icon Persimmon Blackbridge from Press Gang Publishing approached me and three of my collaborators about turning our stage show *Taste This:* into a book. We had just returned from touring the show down the coast to San Francisco, driving Lyndell's foster father's borrowed Honda Civic and eating pasta salad that we dangerously stored unrefrigerated in the trunk for six days straight, and sleeping on couches of ex-girlfriends and ex-girlfriends of ex-girlfriends. None of us had even imagined publishing a book. We had absolutely no clue what we were doing. In order for me to submit a manuscript, I had to transcribe some of my stories from memory first. Some of my pieces from that show existed only as crib notes, scrawled on the back of flaps off of packs of my then-beloved Player's Light Regular cigarettes. I was the oldest of the four of us when we first started working on that book—twenty-seven and working as an electrician.

We were so elated and flabbergasted to be publishing a real-life book with an actual publisher. No one stopped to read the contract, or to even think about the fine print. These were heady times, and even knowing what I know now—that Press Gang would eventually file for bankruptcy, and we would never see a penny of royalties—I would do it all over again, and not change a single thing.

But thirteen books and nearly thirty years later, I read Chelene Knight's *Safekeeping* and found myself moved to tears at least once every chapter.

Of course this book never existed thirty years ago, and even if it had, it probably wouldn't have appeared on my radar, my path to publishing being as unusual and random as it was then, and kind of still is. I went to the British Columbia Institute of Technology and studied electricity and industrial electronics. I didn't go to university and do a master's in creative writing. I never made writer friends in my fourth-year writing workshop. I made it all up as I went along, and as I read every page of this thoughtful, compassionate, and ever-so-sage guided workbook, I cried. What if someone had told me thirty years ago how to better care for myself and my heart and my health and my creative soul as I navigated writing, publishing, and especially touring and promoting my books? My blood, my every spare minute, my sacrifice of so many other things I could have been doing, my stories. The stories of my life.

After *Taste This:* was published in 1998, won an American Library Association Award, sold out its first edition, and was reprinted, and after the publisher sold the rights to a much bigger and more mainstream publisher who discontinued it, and sent my remaindered copies back to me (they sat in the rain for two days on my back porch because I was on the road for a gig, and the top-of-the-box copies swelled up like bloated bellies and I had to toss them out), I kept on writing, and getting up on any and every stage that would have me. Soon after, I was at a gig at the Mighty Niagara, and Blaine Kyllo from Arsenal Pulp Press slipped me his business card. Did I want to send them a solo manuscript? I went on to publish eleven books with Arsenal Pulp Press. I know, I know. I'm lucky, right?

Well, lucky—and I do a lot of live gigs.

You know those Facebook memories? Where they tell you where you were and what you said you were up to on this day for the last however many years? Mine always tell me I was somewhere, rarely at home, and that I had just finished a great show, but that I was tired. Or sick. Or I was leaving too soon the next day, or on the couch recovering from wherever I had just been before I had to go wherever it was I had to go next.

As I read *Safekeeping*, and rode the waves of feelings this insightful book and the advice it contains brought up in me, I didn't think if I had to do it all over again, I would do different things, but I know for certain that I would do many of the same things so much differently.

I would think about and acknowledge the toll that writing and performing and talking about trans and queer issues took and continues to take on my writer's heart. On my tender and yet so tenacious vagus nerve. On this one and only body I have.

I would more easily, and with more certainty and clarity, say no to the gigs I didn't feel aligned with my morals and principles and internal scales of justice.

I would give a wider berth to the folks flying their ragged flags of unfocused rage and trauma, even if I recognized shadows of my own in them.

I would take more time to rest and recuperate. I would say no more, and earlier, and with so much more kindness and compassion for the asker, and for myself.

I would value my work and my time and my art and experience more, and sooner. I would remember to thank my writer friends faster and more often.

I published my most recent book with McClelland and Stewart. I was lucky again, and got to work with great people, but even with one of the top five big Canadian publishers, I am still responsible for my own tours, for my own side hustles, for my own care and feeding and emotional safety. Taking care of the writer is still primarily the job of the writer.

The good news is, I am not finished writing and publishing and touring, and I have *Safekeeping* now, and I know in my bones that it will help me do the same things so much differently.

And you. You have *Safekeeping* now, too. Read it. Think about it. Write in it. Let it be a vessel, a portal, a place to honour and hold your writer's heart.

This book will help you write your next book and, even more importantly, the one after that, too. This book will encourage you to steer yourself with intention through the process of publishing and touring your work and excelling at the business of being a writer, while keeping your boundaries and your politics and yourself alive and breathing.

Yes, this world needs your words. This world also needs you to be healthy, and rested, and ready and able to keep on being a writer. This world needs you to take care of the creator in you.

Ivan Coyote
September 2024

YOUR JOURNAL DEDICATION

I dedicate this journal to

____

____

because

____

____

____

Welcome!

As a writer, you deserve to be heard, to feel safe, and to experience joy while creating and throughout your entire publishing journey. I've examined my own experiences and realized that the foundation authors need to sustain long-term careers wasn't being built, prioritized, or widely talked about, or at least not in a way that encouraged them to consider who they are and what's really important to them as writers. This journal will help you put yourself and your heart work (your writing) first and give you the tools you need to engage with all the parts of yourself that make you the amazing writer you are.

It all starts and ends with how you value yourself as a writer.

Your inner critic is always going to be voicing her opinion, so focusing on what you value about yourself can help quiet that critic. Part of building self-worth is accepting and appreciating who you are and what you have.

Create a list of five things that make you awesome. From that list, pick one that connects to who you are as a writer.

1. ____________________

2. ____________________

3. ____________________

4. ____________________

5. ____________________

I value myself as a writer because

I hope this guided journal can do four things to help you build the foundation for an intentional creative career with you at the centre.

1. **Guide** you through the dreaming phase of your book.
2. **Clarify** your brand and how you want to show up as an author.
3. **Build** a unique and intentional plan for publishing when the time is right.
4. **Act** as a keepsake of the entire experience to help you value the incredible work it takes to be a writer.

Mark This Journal Up!

Engage with the text, underline and highlight important points, mark up the pages with notes, ideas, and questions. Give yourself space to disagree, too. Feel free to revise the language throughout this journal. If you come across a word or phrase that doesn't feel right, cross it out and insert something else. But write down *why* it doesn't work for you so that when you reread the journal you can see what's changed for you and what hasn't. Watch how this contributes to your confidence!

Where to Start?

This journal is divided into three parts: **Before Publishing**, **Publishing**, and **After Publishing**. Much like starting a new writing project, knowing where to begin is important. Where you begin marks the start of your own unique path. And sometimes where you start is also where you end. You can decide where to start based on where you are in your writing journey. Whether you are working on a draft and just penned your first page, or whether you've already launched your book (or books!), this journal is for you.

Fun fact: If publishing is *not* your end goal, that's okay! This journal is still for you. It focuses mostly on the dreaming of your book and book experience as well as the preparation. Maybe publishing *is* your end goal, but you're just not there yet. That's okay, too. You can start with the part that best suits your current phase of writing and then move forward from there. Or you can work on the journal out of order! You can always come back to the publishing part later, but there is plenty of preparatory work you can do in the meantime. I will often ask you to refer to previous parts because some of the exercises build on one another.

Remember, this journal is also meant to be a keepsake. It is a way to look back and pat yourself on the back, and a way to learn from the moments that didn't go as planned. **And you can have one for each and every book you're working on!**

On the next page are some suggestions for where to begin based on your current situation. Of course, you can work through the journal in whatever way feels right for you and your journey.

1. **You're working on multiple book projects.** Pick one book project to prioritize with this journal. In the space below, write why you want to prioritize this project. Then move on to situation two.

2. **You're drafting your manuscript and don't have a publisher yet.** If you're drafting your book but don't have a publisher yet, or publishing is not currently your goal, start from the very beginning of this journal. You can work through the journal and skip **Part 2: Publishing**, and carry on to **Part 3: After Publishing**. While you're here, take a moment to note why publishing is *not* a goal for you. It's important to have clarity here.

3. **You've signed with a publisher and you're in the editing phase.** If you've signed with a publisher and you're early in the journey, you *can* start with the **Dream** chapter, but it would make more sense to begin with the **Discover** chapter and save the **Dream** chapter for your next project. Or you can start by going back and forth between the two chapters. Not everything in the **Dream** chapter will apply, but give it a skim!

4. **You've signed with a publisher and you're in the marketing and publicity phase.** If you've signed with a publisher and you're starting to work on visibility, you can start with the **Learn** chapter and move forward from here. Skim the **Dream** and **Discover** chapters so you know what to expect for your next project.

5. **Your book is out there and you're touring.** Start with the **Keep Safe** chapter at the end of the journal, and then dive *immediately* into the beginning of the journal to vision your next project with clarity!

How to Use Your Journal

Throughout the journal, I'll ask you to focus on the things you have control over; our minds like to naturally drift to the things we don't. When you can focus on the things you do have control over, such as the way you respond to a situation, what you say yes to, or who you share your writing with, you'll begin to feel more in control of your writing life—and life in general.

Here are the tasks that repeat in each chapter of the journal:

INTENTIONS

In each chapter, I will ask you to set an intention for yourself, as well as for your book. An intention is meant to serve as an entry point into assessing what you want for your experience. An intention is not a goal but an attitude that you want to experience in the moment. Each passing day, you'll feel differently about where you stand with your book. One day, you might feel solid, confident, and eager to share it with others, whereas the next day, you might contemplate throwing years of work into the ocean and renouncing the title of writer. Yes, it can be that drastic! Therefore, having an intention each time you dive into the journal will help you meet yourself where you are at that moment.

For example: *Today I want to be curious and learn something new about myself as a writer.*

This is a great intention because it's broad, which promotes flexibility, and it's easily attained. Anything else you achieve is a bonus.

Here's another one: *I want to enter into this section of the journal with an open mind and challenge myself to think differently.*

AFFIRMATIONS

In each chapter, I will also ask you to write affirmations. An affirmation can be any positive or even factual statement that resonates with you. When you lean into affirmations with an open mind, they can help you build, or rebuild, the narrative you tell yourself about who you are as a writer. These narratives are stories that we have absorbed over time that eventually become beliefs. For example, we might believe we can't call ourselves a writer if we haven't published yet. But we can use affirmations to remind ourselves that a writer is someone who enjoys being immersed in the consistent sculpting of their work, and that story will eventually take up the most space in your head and become a new belief. As you construct a new story for yourself and your book, you'll have more clarity and confidence. You'll also start to build self-trust as a writer, and that, my friend, is priceless. When you find yourself in a room full of people all talking about you as a writer, your voice will be the one you'll hear loudest, so controlling the self-narrative is key to your growth.

For example: *Language is my superpower and I can tell a story in vivid ways.*

or

I can change other people's way of seeing things with what I write.

Sometimes our belief systems need to be jostled. They need to earn their space in our heads. And if they don't, we have to Let. Them. Go.

3 TIPS

Not gonna lie, these are probably my favourite sections in the journal. As busy writers who have other obligations and life responsibilities, we sometimes need a quick takeaway to put into action immediately. Instant gratification shouldn't be our end goal, but giving ourselves a tool to use right away can be such a sweet gift when everything else in our writerly lives is moving so slowly. Feel free to dive right into these tips or flag them for later. Pay attention to how you feel when you read the tips. If you feel a surge of inspiration, lean into it, y'all, because these can be few and far between. If you experience a little resistance, that's okay, too. You'll find ways to come back.

WRITING PROMPTS

It's time to flex your writerly muscles! Each chapter includes a writing prompt meant to help you go deeper into your writer's toolbox to use and grow the skills you already hold. These prompts aren't meant to make you write anything publishable, but they can unlock a new superpower, dream, or goal. Each writing prompt is an opportunity to slow down, tap into **Your Why** (page 43), and surprise yourself.

EXERCISES

The exercises are different from the writing prompts in that they will ask you to step *away* from the writing and tackle your mindset. These exercises will help you build self-trust so that you can trust not only the process in this journal but, more importantly, the decisions you make for yourself and your books.

REFLECTIONS

Reflecting doesn't come naturally to many of us, and sometimes we already come to the table jaded or with a negative view of the act of reflecting. Most of us are taught *not* to look back, to just keep pressing forward. But without reflecting, we cannot change, grow, or track our progress. So this journal offers you moments for reflection in the hope that you can make it a part of your regular daily life. Learning to slow down and assess is a tool that will serve you well throughout your writing career. Publishing moves slowly until it doesn't. You'll blink and it'll be over. Writing a book and publishing it are both experiences worthy of celebration. Celebrate your book by giving yourself an opportunity to look back at all the work you've done, the people you've met, the stumbling blocks, the milestones, the teary moments, the times you wanted to quit, and the moments when you had to pinch yourself. In addition to helping you clarify who you are as a writer, this journal will help you build an honest time capsule for you to look back on and even help you prepare for your next book and all the books to follow.

Chelene's Vault

By reflecting on my own unique experiences publishing my books, I started to see patterns (some good, some not so good), and I was able to pinpoint the changes I wanted to make with my next book experience, and the next. I took control over my projects and began to build stronger, more cooperative relationships with my publishing peers. I found so much value in the work I was doing in the publishing world and how it was changing and inspiring others. This ultimately led me to build a more recognizable brand, which I can refine over time. In my post-event reflections, I could see that the conversations I was having about my books were conversations that I *wanted* to be having. When we zero in on what our message is and what we want to present to the world, and then protect it, magic happens. Through this holistic approach, I learned how to amplify my voice, and most importantly, I learned how to build an intentional process for saying no with love. I was then able to curate the creative life of my dreams. I could also see that the more I worked on myself personally, the more it benefited my professional life, especially my coaching practice.

You'll learn more about me throughout this journal in the sidebars from inside **Chelene's Vault**!

The Safe

Welcome to the **Safe**! What new knowledge now holds value to you? Tuck it away here. This is the place where you can drop off valuable learnings, milestones, epiphanies, and writing breakthroughs, as well as quotes that you collect over the course of filling in your journal. There's nothing like seeing yourself or your situation in another writer's experience! Every time you come across quotes in the journal, or in the world from various writers, slow down and ask yourself, "How can I see myself here?" Feel free to make a note right under the quote itself if you feel inspired. And don't worry, I'll remind you often to lock something precious in your safe.

The Inventory

The **Inventory** is your toolbox. It's a place for you to take stock of your current writer collaborators. The Inventory is different from the Safe because these are tools you already have, the community you can call in and lean on, and the skills you've acquired. When imposter syndrome starts to seep in (and it will), we can lean on our Inventory for support.

Time to show yourself some love! Remind yourself that you're a writer, that you've invested time and energy into yourself and your craft. In each box below, begin to document your writerly inventory. You can always come back and add more items as you work through the journal, but go ahead and get started. This will help you acknowledge and appreciate at a glance all the wonderful support you already have.

My tangible writerly collaborators

Transferable skills I've acquired over the years

My communities

Praise and love I've received

My favourite quotes

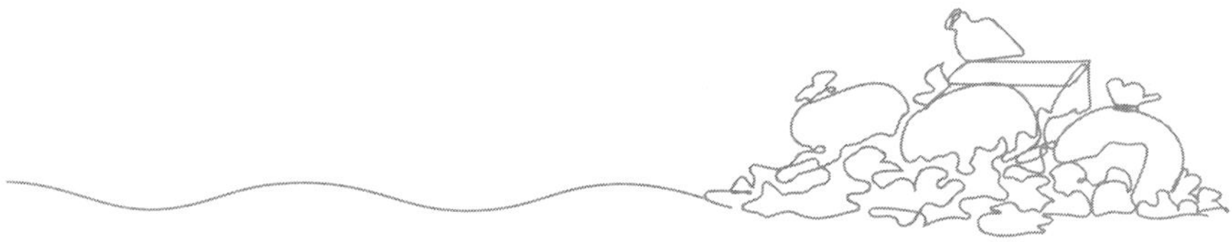

The Mind Dump

LET IT GO

The **Mind Dump** is the place where you can drop off negative feelings, old learnings and beliefs that no longer serve you, and anything else that is blocking your writerly journey. The phrase “Let it go!” is your reminder to head back to the Mind Dump and drop off any anxiety, drama, or unneeded baggage. I’ll remind you to let go often. Remember, any time you drop something off acts as an acknowledgement that there is something that no longer fits in your life. Letting go is complex, lifelong work. But the Mind Dump can help you get started. This is the perfect way to start your journey feeling a bit lighter. Are you ready?

Writer's Block

Controversial opinion: I don't think writer's block exists. I think writer's block—a phrase used by almost every writer who's ever experienced the mind-boggling pain of the blank page—is an excuse we rely on to give us permission to stop what we're doing. Writer's block also allows us to ignore the underlying issues that may be causing the feeling of being stuck. If you get stuck working on a section of this book or on your own book project, slow down and assess what you might need in that moment. The feeling of being stuck is often connected to either something in your writing process that is no longer working for you or your body or brain asking for something. Listen to this call and try asking the following questions:

Do you need a drink of water, food, a stretch?

Do you need to change an aspect of your current writing process? For example, I used to only write late at night, but this no longer works for me since I have a very different work schedule, so I let go of that old part of my process.

Is there a bigger personal problem tugging at you? What can you mine from this data?

Can you take some breathing space and try again in a few minutes?

Is your energy spent? Maybe you just need to take a break and do something else.

Breaking Barriers and Embracing Diversity

In the writing and publishing industries, privilege and access have long played a pivotal role in determining who gets to share their voices and stories with the world. Traditionally, publishing has been a realm guarded by gatekeepers, shrouded in opacity, and often favouring archaic practices that push underrepresented authors to the margins. This has perpetuated a cycle of inequality in storytelling, where voices from marginalized communities struggle to be heard.

I've seen the insides of publishing from some of the most nuanced angles, and I've built a seat for myself at many of the tables that, for a variety of reasons, have been systemically off limits to a young woman of colour writer who had very different ideas of the tools that should be available to writers.

However, diverse voices are beginning to break through. This journal aspires to be a guide for all writers, but it is definitely a necessary tool for marginalized creators. So, as you work through this guided journal, remember that your unique perspective is a source of strength. Make note of the people and resources that can help you overcome barriers. Barriers might include difficulty finding a publisher or editor who understands your voice, not having access to certain entry points in publishing, or just not feeling safe. Imagine yourself on a journey through the pages of your creative life. As you hit roadblocks or feel like certain doors are locked, take a moment to lean into that discomfort. Perhaps drop those heavy barriers off in the **Mind Dump** (page 15). Consider them challenges to be navigated, rather than insurmountable obstacles. You might find resources to help you overcome these barriers in friends, mentors, or organizations dedicated to fostering inclusivity and diversity in the creative space. Add these to the **Safe** (page 10). It's essential to remember that you don't have to navigate this journey alone. Communities and support systems exist to guide you in your creative endeavours.

It's crucial for *all* creators to pause, reflect on, and acknowledge the aspects of writing and publishing that might currently feel inaccessible and why. You'll notice that slowing down is a repeated theme in this journal. These moments of reflection are not signs of weakness but rather opportunities for growth and transformation. Like anyone, I've made a lot of mistakes, such as working with the wrong people, rushing, not asking questions...the list goes on. The good news is that these mistakes have become learning opportunities and catalysts for some of the positive changes we are now seeing in the industry.

Your story matters. Now, let's start building a beautiful home for it!

Part 1

Before Publishing

I dream a dream that dreams back at me.
—Toni Morrison, *A Mercy*

Chapter 1

Dream

This chapter is your opportunity to think outside the box, to push yourself, and to call in your imagination. Explore all the possibilities and take your time thinking big. Imagine that all the rules and rigid expectations melt away. What do you see?

DREAM *Intention and Affirmation*

My intention for this chapter is to

The affirmation I will say to myself throughout this chapter to hold up that intention is

DREAM *Your Definition of Success*

When I look back at my early days as a writer, there's one thing that I wish someone would have told me because I now see how it could have changed my life: *Define success for yourself.* I remember having a conversation with a writer friend about our writing lives. We sat down for coffee and she briefly mentioned that she was upset that her book was not successful. We sat in silence for a minute until I asked her what her definition of success was. She didn't have an answer. It was the thirty seconds of silence that followed that made me realize how important this dreaming work is. We have to make this journey make sense for *us*. Perhaps her definition of success was tethered to what she saw other writers experiencing. It's difficult *not* to compare ourselves to other writers. She was probably focusing only on book sales and publicity—numbers and visibility. She had skipped building her own map for a successful book.

Success is personal, and it's essential that each writer defines and sculpts success as an individual, with distinct lived experiences and goals. For each book you write, you should dream a definition of success in order to track your progress and grow with each and every book. Fun fact: You should revise your definition of success for each book, until eventually, you've found your footing, your brand, and how you want to show up for the rest of your writerly career.

My own definitions of success for my books were all different, but each one was intricately connected to how I wanted to show up as an author. I didn't even start thinking about that until book three, so that's when my definition of success really changed. My new definition of success was to talk about love and care in unexpected ways and be invited to shed light on what can happen when you protect your energy. With book three, I started to say no—a lot. There were events, projects, and organizations that did not align with my new definition of success. And that definition hasn't changed much since, thanks to the clarity that came when I slowed down long enough to pay attention.

Here are some considerations to help you dream your definition of success for this book:

- **Conversations.** What do you want to talk about and how does it connect to who you are? How can having these conversations change beliefs? How can you put yourself in the right spaces for these conversations to take place?
- **Community.** Who do you think will benefit from your story the most? What ripples can you imagine coming from you connecting with these people and groups? This is the starting point for defining your audience.
- **Collaborations.** What would it look and feel like to partner with people you admire? How does your message connect to theirs? Who might help you build visibility?

When it comes to my book ______________________________,
I define success as

____

____

____

____

____

____

____

____

DREAM *Your Ideal Experience*

You can dream the ideal experience for every stage of your book journey: the drafting, revising, publishing, and promotion. It's 100 percent up to you. Think about your **Inventory** (page 12): What and who do you see tagging along with you on this journey? What would it look like, feel like, taste like to build your book and appreciate this current experience? Be as specific as possible and, hey, this *is* the **Dream** chapter, so get wild and bold!

My ideal (drafting, revising, publishing) ______________________ experience:

____

____

____

____

____

____

____

____

____

____

____

Is there something you want to keep safe and protect? Lovingly drop it off in the **Safe** (page 10). Is there anything you want to let go of? Leave it in the **Mind Dump** (page 15).

Chelene's Vault

When I started promoting my third book, *Junie*, I had big dreams. My biggest dream was that my book would be adapted for film—and it's now in the process of being adapted into a TV series. For my fourth book, *Let It Go*, I really wanted to be invited to New York—no dice yet! Dreams don't always come true, but we certainly give them a better chance if we know what they are in the first place. When dreaming your ideal experience, allow yourself to imagine beyond what you have been told is possible.

DREAM *Letter to Your Book Project*

Any time you want to prioritize something and recognize its value, I recommend that you build an emotional narrative around it. An emotional narrative is a story you tell yourself about your non-negotiables—your boundaries or priorities—in order to make them stick. An emotional narrative can look like telling yourself what your life would be like *without* that non-negotiable in place. You can also imagine a life with that non-negotiable firmly intact. The best way I know to start building an emotional narrative is to write a letter. Writing letters is personal. The act can be unstructured if you let yourself write what you're feeling in the moment. Letters are a piece of you in the present. Imagine your book to be a good friend, a loved one, a partner. What would you want your book to know about you and your writerly dreams? How is your book a part of who you are?

3 TIPS *For Working on More than One Book at a Time*

Over the years I've figured out that it takes different parts of my brain (and heart) to research, draft, and revise a book. When working on multiple projects in different genres and in different phases of writing, I don't feel overwhelmed but invigorated, as if my entire brain is working at full capacity. But when you're working on multiple projects, balance is key. You don't want to overload your brain with too much of one thing. You want to be able to flow freely from one project to the next. So here are three tips for working on more than one book at a time:

1. **Make sure your projects are in different phases of the writing process.** I consider there to be three general yet distinct phases of writing: unstructured play, drafting, and revision. There can be an unlimited number of sub-categories, such as research and interviews, depending on the project, but when you have projects in different phases, they require you to use different parts of your brain instead of overloading one. I never have more than one project in drafting mode because it takes so much energy from me.

2. **Know when you're most creative or analytical and schedule your writing sessions accordingly.** For example, if you're a night owl, what type of writing seems to flow at this time? Is it creativity and unstructured play, like mind mapping? Or is it deeply researched content? Does your brain immediately jump into the sculpting phase of revision? What aspects of your living situation allow for this kind of process? Knowing where you shine and when will help you prioritize which project to work on at what time. This also allows you to have more control over the production of your work—you begin creating on your terms. You'll figure out when to best focus on the "business" side of writing depending on what you discover about that analytical brain! Your habits, schedule, and living

situation can change over time, which is why it's important to evaluate your writing process seasonally and make adjustments.

3. **Have clear entry and exit points for your writing session.** There's nothing worse than having trouble getting started, or not being able to crawl out of a writing session to meet the rest of your appointments, work, and obligations. What can you use to trigger the start of a session? How will you end your session? Consider what you know to be true about yourself and let that inform your entry and exit strategies. When I'm doing research, I often get lost down rabbit holes, so I have a loud timer that brings me back and reminds me that it's time to switch tasks. Brainstorm what might work for you below:

WRITING PROMPT *Get Inside Your Character's Head*

Imagine your main character has a secret. It can be super personal, embarrassing, or even joyful. But make it a big secret. Something unexpected of your character. Now, write a diary entry in your character's voice without ever directly disclosing the secret. This is an opportunity to play with interiority. It will help you to not only get to know more about your character but also to get closer to their voice and how they would say all the things they'd never say out loud. Remember, there are characters no matter the genre, including memoir and even poetry.

EXERCISE *Dream Your Own Book Blurb*

Now that you've flexed your emotional muscles, it's time to big yourself up! What are all things you dream of folks saying about your book? What do you want your readers to take away? Who do you want to say these glowing things about your book? Again, this space to dream can be so powerful. Dreaming and joy are intrinsic to your process and development as a writer. So go ahead, pass yourself the mic and write a blurb written in the voice of your favourite author.

BONUS CHALLENGE

Write a list of all the potential authors who could realistically blurb your book in the future. Consider authors you might have a connection with either directly or indirectly. Asking authors to endorse your book can bring about a little anxiety. It's a lot to ask of an already busy creative, so planning early will help reduce this anxiety. And be sure to prepare for the nos. Chances are, many seasoned writers have been working on protecting their energy, and they might say no with love. So make your list robust!

What would you say in an email to one of those authors? Consider your personal connection, why you selected them, and all the necessary information, like where to send their blurb, the blurb deadline, and anything else they might need to make an informed decision.

Reflection

Be Kind, but Be Honest

A consistent reflection practice will allow you to track your personal growth, because when you look back you will be able to pinpoint what's changed and what you've learned. Spend a few minutes reflecting on how you feel about the materials you worked through in the **Dream** chapter. What surprises you? What excites you? What scares you? Write like no one will ever read this.

CHECK-IN CORNER *Let Go and Keep Safe*

Do any of the above points push against or challenge what you've been told about writing? Is there something in your writing process that you'll now have to change? You can drop it off in the **Mind Dump** (page 15). Is there anything that you learned that you want to add to your **Inventory** (page 12) or something valuable to protect in your **Safe** (page 10)?

We write for the same reason that we walk, talk, climb mountains or swim the oceans—because we can. We have some impulse within us that makes us want to explain ourselves to other human beings.
—Maya Angelou

Chapter 2

Discover

It's time to get curious! In this chapter, you'll build a robust toolkit for your book project. You'll gain clarity about why your book is important to you and what you hope it will do in the world. Get ready for lots of surprises!

DISCOVER *Intention and Affirmation*

My intention for this chapter is to

The affirmation I will say to myself throughout this chapter to hold up that intention is

DISCOVER *Your Why*

Discovering a clear purpose—your why—behind your writing journey is pivotal. Not only does it guide your decisions regarding your current book, but it also shapes the trajectory of your entire writing career. Your why serves as the compass that directs you to the opportunities you embrace, the promotional strategies you choose, and even your approach to future projects. Understanding your why is invaluable! Take your time with this one. There's no deadline here.

There are two different whys to explore:

1. Why do you write?
2. Why are you writing this specific book?

Start thinking about why you write. This will probably be an emotional experience (it certainly is for me), but let yourself fall into it. Before you can trust me, you have to trust yourself, and trust is a difficult thing. When I describe my own why, I've learned that writing is an extension of who I am. If I can't write, I'm not myself. So get cozy with reflection and difficult questions! Take a few moments here to brainstorm on *why* you write:

Take that why one step further and connect it to your specific book project. Acknowledging why you wrote, or are writing, this book is one of the most important steps a writer can take. Knowing your why will help you make intentional decisions and will play a strong role in your book's transformations and how you show up. Your why will inform the people you reach. Knowing your why can intimately lead to a more joyful writing and publishing experience.

Now, refine your why using the prompts below:

I am writing ______________________________ because

If ______________________________ didn't exist, I would feel

____

____

____

____

____

I am the best person to write ______________________ because

____

____

____

____

____

Reminder: Add your why to your **Inventory** (page 12).

Chelene's Vault

When I was drafting my novel, *Junie*, I was clear that my why was that I am writing this book to shed light on the living and loving between various ambitious Black women that took place in the now demolished neighbourhood called Hogan's Alley in Vancouver. Because I was clear on my why, working with my editor was a breeze, because if she made suggestions that steered me away from my why, we could have an informed conversation that brought us back. I could easily share my reasons for not incorporating some of her suggested changes because I understood my why. Bonus: My why made it very clear to me what types of events I should be saying yes to.

DISCOVER *Your Book's Action*

What is your book's action? What do you want it to do in the world? Any time I ask authors this question they almost always hit me with a long, slow pause. But I encourage this act of slowing down because once you solidify your book's action, combined with your personal why, the decisions you make about and adjacent to your book become easier, intentional, and empowering. When you know what you want your book to do in the world, you suddenly become quite clear about what spaces you need to be in and what conversations you need to have about your book. This action will make sure you get your book into the right hands.

If your book's action is to create a conversation with youth about identity, for example, then how can you make sure your book (and you) show up in the spaces where these conversations would take place? What themes from your book contribute to this action? What decisions can you then make with this information? With my latest book, *Let It Go: Free Yourself from Old Beliefs and Find a New Path to Joy*, it was very important to me that I temporarily step away from the literary spaces I was used to and stand in front of a new audience. I wanted to have conversations with psychotherapists, folks working in wellness centres and mental health organizations, and other spaces where my book's message, why, and action could be best absorbed. Because I was very clear about this, it was a lot easier for me to say yes to these opportunities and no to others. I was also clear about who I should pitch myself to because I knew what my message was and who I wanted to receive it.

Brainstorm your book's action below:

___

___

___

Extract one clear action from your brainstorm and compose one concise sentence:

My example for *Let It Go*:

I want my book to debunk the thinking that life needs to be without pain in order for us to experience joy, because the difficult living is the reason we need joy.

DISCOVER *The Three B's*

The Three B's are tools meant to help you understand your unique value as a writer:

- **Be** in competition with previous versions of yourself
- **Big** yourself up
- **Bust** out your superpower

BE *in Competition with Previous Versions of Yourself*

It's natural to compare yourself to other authors, but it's not helpful. With the rise of social media, it's hard to ignore our peers attending events we didn't get invited to or being shortlisted for awards we didn't get nominated for. But remember your definition of success, your why, and your book's action. These are the things that make your book publishing experience uniquely yours. Here are some ways to overtake your fiercest competitor—yourself!

- **Track your growth:** Where were you last year? What new learnings or experiences have you gained?
    - Create a personal development tracker: How have you invested time and energy in yourself? You can use a spreadsheet (or medium of your choice) to track all the books you've read, courses you've taken, workshops you've participated in, and more.
- **Write a book bucket list:** What are all the activities you hope to be a part of because your book exists in the world? Even if these things don't happen, they're still something to continue to work toward.

- **Make a list of what to focus on:** What do you have control over? Push everything else out of view. For example, you have control over:
    - The conversations you decide to have.
    - What you share about your writing process.
    - Who you let read early drafts.

BIG *Yourself Up*

Writing a book is no easy feat. Big yourself up! We can't expect those around us to lift us up if we aren't willing to do it for ourselves. Create a list of five things that make you awesome. Be bold! Be honest! Imagine if someone close to you wrote this list about you and handed it to you. You'd be shocked, you'd feel incredible, and maybe you'd even get a little emotional. Heck, you can even pull out your CV and remind yourself of all that you've accomplished. Use this list when you're feeling a bit down about how an event went, or not getting that one specific invite. This is a small yet powerful exercise. And using it consistently will help you build a new more positive narrative about who you are. At first, you might only be able to come up with a few things that make you awesome. Over time, it will come more naturally. But think about all the little things that contribute to who you are, even if they aren't connected to writing. Here are a few of my own examples:

- I have a great sense of humour (with the right people!).
- I can cook anything, even without a recipe.
- I can predict what's going to happen next in a movie.
- I can help writers feel good about their projects.
- I am great at helping writers find a unique "shape" for their books.

1. ______________________________

2. ______________________________

3. ______________________________

4. ______________________________

5. ______________________________

BUST *Out Your Superpower*

No, I'm not suggesting you put on a flowy red cape and tights and leap tall buildings in a single bound. That's not the kind of superpower I'm talking about! What is something you do well and in such a unique way that it feels like a superpower? This trait could even be something connected to a characteristic that you once saw as a flaw. How can this be used to promote your book? What other ways can it be used?

How to find your superpower:

1. Think about a characteristic that allows you to show up as your authentic self. For example, maybe you talk a lot, maybe you have a bold sense of humour, maybe you are loud, maybe you move slowly, maybe you overthink things, or maybe you rush.
2. Make a list of the good that has come to you from that characteristic.
3. Make a list of the good that has come to others through that characteristic.
4. Think about the role you want to have in the creative world.
5. Find a link between the characteristic and your creative goal.

6. Write your superpower statement, including the positive effect on yourself and others.

Here's my example:

Deep listening is my superpower! Being an introvert allows me to work with other writers because I can dig deep and ask big questions of their creative work. Folks who work with me experience big surprises and leaps in progress and feel more connected to their process.

Set a timer for twenty minutes to brainstorm about your potential superpower knowing there are no wrong answers. Be open. Be honest. Be curious.

Write your superpower statement:

Chelene's Vault

By the time I started promoting my fourth book, *Let It Go*, I realized I hadn't been experiencing the level of joy I should have with the previous few books. Things had to change! I had so much to offer the world but was afraid to assert myself; perhaps I was afraid to be seen. When I thought about my superpower, I was shocked to learn it was my introversion, which distilled into deep listening skills. How could I put this to work for me and my book? Let's just say, this shift changed my career and book publishing experience for the better. And I found my footing as a coach because listening is one of the most coveted skills in the field.

As part of my Thrive Coaching Program, I ask my creatives to investigate their superpower and we speak about it one-on-one. A previous client had such a strong emotional reaction to her superpower that it changed her manuscript, her approach, her career direction, and even her joy. And I got to witness that. In that moment, I knew she was going to do big things. It was a feeling I could sense crawling through my bones. We all need that feeling. As writers, we chase it.

My newfound deep listening superpower also transformed my perspective on moderating events. I realized that it wasn't that I disliked moderation, which is what I had believed for ten years; rather, I preferred to engage in intentional conversations and craved the intimacy of one-on-one interactions. This realization prompted me to proudly showcase it as an additional strength in my speaking career. Through this introspective journey, I've had the privilege of engaging in one-on-one discussions with renowned authors like acclaimed poet Ross Gay, two-time Giller Prize winner Esi Edugyan, and Pulitzer Prize winner Natasha Trethewey. This superpower is now a powerful tool in my author brand toolkit!

3 TIPS *For Using Your Authentic Voice on the Page*

We hear the word *voice* everywhere when it comes to writing, but what does it even mean? Voice is informed by how you experience the world around you and how you document that experience on the page. There are so many things in our life that influence voice. Do we have control over our voice? Can our voice evolve and change? Can we have more than one voice? To show up authentically, you have to go inward. You have to get to know what your style is and how to highlight it on the page. Think about your personality and how you speak in real life. What does this say about you? How can you call in who you really are and use it as a megaphone for your message? Here are three tips for getting your authentic voice on the page:

1. **Read widely, inside and outside your genre.** This is probably the tip that gave me the most benefit. Reading anything from obscure poetry to historical fiction to home design books is what helped me see all the links between the various genres. I could shapeshift my voice in my writing depending on what book I was reading. Be open to exploring other types of books and lean in with curiosity. Ask questions! Write in the margins! Well, as long as they aren't library books.

2. **Dissect the style of writers you admire.** Take tip one a bit further by choosing an author you love and dissecting their writing style. I had a discussion with a friend about what it would be like to take a favourite-writer-themed writing retreat where we immersed ourselves in that writer's work, be it their books, articles, interviews, or documentaries. How could we learn everything we could about them? How could we ask important questions of their work and our own?

3. **Embrace the mess. Edit later.** Before sitting down to write, remind yourself that it is going to be messy but there will be ample and intentional time for you to edit. It can be difficult

to turn off the internal editor when you're writing, but in order to keep the authentic flow and momentum going, you need to let the writing hit the page as it comes. Don't break that flow. How do you envision your own revision process and rituals taking shape?

Chelene's Vault

When I first started out as a writer, my mentor at the time spoke often about how initial drafts are supposed to be messy. He used an analogy of building a car and how you had to gather pieces like the doors, engine, and bumper. These car pieces might cover an entire room, and you probably didn't even know the names of most of them, let alone how they fit together! And as much as you were excited to hop in the driver's seat, you couldn't drive the car until you figured out how to put it together. And that's really what writing is. We are putting these cars together, always looking for new ways to do it. This is what excites me about writing. I've come to embrace the art of revision because it allows me to witness instant improvements, whether it's tweaking a single line or reshaping an opening paragraph. I am forever in search of that aha moment when I know I'm doing something that just works. When I wrote my novel, *Junie*, I underwent seventeen rounds of revision, yet each pass felt deliberate and essential to the creative journey.

WRITING PROMPT *Write a Snapshot in Time*

Find a familiar photo and spend a few moments observing it, letting your mind wander. Imagine what could have happened just five minutes before that snapshot was taken. Dive into the setting, envision the dialogue, and tune in to the overall tone of those moments. Now, let your imagination loose and start free writing about those captivating pre-photo moments.

EXERCISE *Change Your Environment*

The space around you influences how you create. It can also encourage a sense of calm. Can you rejig your writing space to call in all the things that inspire you? Maybe you can declutter your desk and pull together a stack of your favourite books and keep them close. Maybe you can change the lighting or incorporate a calming colour. Outline your plan to update your environment and make your space uniquely yours.

Reflection

Be Kind, but Be Honest

A consistent reflection practice will allow you to track your personal growth, because when you look back at your reflections you will be able to pinpoint what's changed and what you've learned. Spend a few minutes reflecting on how you feel about the materials you worked through in the **Discover** chapter. What surprises you? What excites you? What scares you? Write like no one will ever read this.

CHECK-IN CORNER *Let Go and Keep Safe*

Did anything surprise you in the **Discover** chapter? You can drop it off in the **Mind Dump** (page 15). Is there anything you need to add to your **Inventory** (page 12) or **Safe** (page 10)?

Notes

I think you write from certain instincts and you write out of your own experience—and you essentially write what's in you.

—Esi Edugyan

Chapter 3

Learn

In this chapter, you'll be going inward a lot and learning new ways to be more intentional about how you use your energy. Move through this chapter with an open mind and an open heart, and you'll feel like your writerly toolkit is that much fuller at the end.

LEARN *Intention and Affirmation*

My intention for this chapter is to

The affirmation I will say to myself throughout this chapter to hold up that intention is

LEARN *How to Celebrate Solo*

Celebration is a learned skill! We aren't thrust into this world knowing how to pat ourselves on the back, or even how to slow down long enough to appreciate the time and effort we've put into something. We are taught from a young age that celebration is about other people. Think back to the first birthday party or holiday engagement you can remember. Who do you see around you? Other people. Learning how to celebrate can be difficult for some because we are often taught to let other people celebrate us. Our brains often default to thinking celebration is selfish, but I hope you can start small and make solo celebration a part of your writing practice.

WHAT IS CELEBRATION?

Every writer must define celebration for themselves. Celebration doesn't have to be reserved for the big things either. For me, celebration is defined as slowing down long enough to say, "I did that, and I'm proud of myself." It can be that simple. Take some time to define what celebration looks like for you:

WHY CELEBRATE SOLO?

Sometimes the internal, private moments attached to drafting a book might not seem worthy of celebration to others. It's important to give yourself an opportunity to hold your joy for each milestone you encounter in your writing journey. It's wonderful to celebrate with others, but start with yourself. This will also build up your confidence and resilience.

WHAT DOES CELEBRATING SOLO HAVE TO DO WITH WRITING?

As writers, we watch time either fly by so quickly that if we blink, it's gone, or crawl by at a painstakingly slow pace. Celebration is a way for us to slow down and appreciate the true experience of writing. *Our* experience of writing. Even writing in this journal is a kind of celebration. It's time invested in yourself and your writing practice. Take a few moments to list some of the ways you might celebrate solo:

Chelene's Vault

Celebrating solo has boosted my confidence in every aspect of my life and nudged me to approach things differently, especially when making big decisions. So much so that in 2020, I made some pretty big life decisions. I ditched my hometown for a small town, went all in on coaching, and finally tackled things I'd been putting off forever, like learning to drive. I made these decisions because I felt like it was time to trust myself even more. I could see what my creative life was becoming, and this gave me the confidence to take some risks in my personal life, too. I felt a push to continue to work on myself, and celebration allowed me the time and space to recognize it.

LEARN *How to Build a Routine*

When you establish a routine around your creative work, it becomes an ingrained part of your daily life. This consistency helps in a few ways. First, it reduces the mental effort required to get started, as the routine cues your brain to shift into creative mode automatically. Second, routines create a sense of accountability, making it less likely for distractions to derail your progress. Third, regular creative routines can improve your skills and productivity over time, as you continually build on your previous work. Overall, cultivating routines around your creative endeavours can provide a stable foundation that fosters focus, boosts creativity, and enhances your ability to see creative projects through to completion. You use less energy when routines are fully formed, and that creative energy can be banked for creative work!

Note: Be kind to yourself—it will take time to build routines. Having routines can also help with decision-making fatigue. When building a routine, connect it to activities you already do without having to think about them.

HOW TO BUILD A POSITIVE ROUTINE

1. List a routine for morning, afternoon, and evening. Reserve the first thirty minutes and the last thirty minutes of your day for you. Dedicating a small chunk of time to *you* is integral to creative and mental health. It reinforces the fact that *you* are important, not just what you do for others.

   Pro tip: It may be helpful to add to your morning routine: *Pick one thing to look forward to at the end of today.* Busy people often zoom through the day without stopping to think or dream about that fun or exciting thing they get to do at the end of the day. When you feel like your workday has no end in sight, think about the activity you're looking forward to. This practice will help you not only move more easily through the day but also stop long enough to appreciate the good things.

2. Add a creative or innovative activity to your morning, afternoon, and evening routines (it can be small!).
3. Check off each activity when it's complete.
4. Once you have your routines built, figure out how much time each activity takes and block it in your calendar!

Here's a sample routine with the creative activities in bold:

Morning

- ✓ Look over financial news with coffee.
- ✓ Flag emails.
- ✓ **Read one poem from my bookshelf.**

Afternoon

- ✓ Take a five-minute walk after lunch.
- ✓ **Pay attention to everything orange outside.**

Evening

- ✓ Stretch for fifteen minutes on my yoga mat.
- ✓ **Free write in my journal for at least fifteen minutes.**
- ✓ Turn off all my devices.

Now build your own routine to support your creative work:

LEARN *How to Thrive*

What does it look like to thrive? It could look like showing up as your best self and being careful about how you spend your energy. It could look like consistently working on yourself so that you eventually find it easier to eliminate all the unhealthy routines and habits you've accumulated over the years. The path to thriving will look different for all of us, but the result is often the same: a healthier, more intentional way of living. Learning how to thrive might be a lifelong endeavour. What does thriving look like to you? Consider not only your writing but also all the other areas in your life that take space, time, and energy from you. What would the experience be like to have everything working together harmoniously? Explore what thriving looks like to you, not only as a writer but as a person in the world today.

Chelene's Vault

In 2023, I built Breathing Space Creative's Thrive Coaching Program, which is an intensive one-on-one program meant to help folks work on themselves in such a way that they organically create the necessary space to do all the things that bring them joy. It started as a program for writers, but I learned that it was actually a program meant for anyone who needed structured support to create the space to live a life filled with all the things that were important to them. Building this program taught me so much about what was possible in terms of personal growth and ditching old beliefs that had been holding me back.

LEARN *How to Say No with Love*

In the days after I finished my creative writing program, I was excited and eager to dive into any writing opportunity that came my way, no matter how small or unrelated to my goals. This was on the advice often given to new writers: say yes to everything, hustle, and gain exposure. Little did I know that this approach could lead to the most intense burnout of my life.

Fast forward a decade, and here I am, finally writing the book I always dreamed of in a way that feels authentic and brings me joy. Saying no with love is at the core of every single piece of self-growth I've experienced. In fact, the outcomes were so booming that I created a free seasonal workshop bearing this very title. I'm steering the ship of my creative journey. This didn't happen by chance. It happened because I developed a process for saying no that was rooted in intentionality, meaning I've thought about why I'm saying no and understand how saying no to a specific ask will preserve my energy. Keep in mind that every time you say yes to one thing, you're implicitly saying no to something else. Take a moment to jot down examples from your own life when you've said no with love and how it had a positive impact on you.

Saying no with love is not easy, but the process is simple. The seven steps to saying no with love become even more exciting the more times you do them because you'll be able to easily track your growth and assess what's changed since the last time. The result of applying these steps is a detailed map that helps you filter opportunities and say no with intention or say yes with conditions.

1. DEFINE HOW YOU WANT TO SHOW UP THIS YEAR

Think about how you want to feel and the spaces you want to be in.

2. SELECT YOUR WORD, LENS, AND THEME FOR THE YEAR

Brainstorm a few ideas, and then commit to one by circling it.

3. OUTLINE YOUR ANNUAL PRIORITIES

What are three to five priorities you want to focus on for the year?

1. ____

2. ____

3. ____

4. ____

5. ____

4. CONDUCT WEEKLY ENERGY ASSESSMENTS

On the next page, create a big list of as many tasks as you can think of that you currently have on your plate. Next, create two lists: one for tasks that suck your energy and one for those that give you energy. Then organize the energy-sucking tasks into three categories:

1. Automate (create a process for)
2. Delegate (give that task to someone else)
3. Eliminate (ditch it altogether)

Tasks

Tasks That Suck Energy

Tasks That Give Energy

Automate

Delegate

Eliminate

5. LET GO OF OLD NARRATIVES AND BELIEF SYSTEMS

This is a big, big process—one that I wrote an entire book on! Work on yourself, shed those unproductive habits, and let go of the conditioning that has shaped you for as long as you can remember. We've all been influenced by the behaviours and beliefs we've absorbed throughout our lives, and breaking free from those patterns requires reflection and mindfulness. List what you want to let go of and why.

---

6. DEVELOP A LOVING LANGUAGE FOR SAYING NO

Developing your language for saying no is a great way to make the no more personal. When building out your say no with love language, pay attention to who you are right now. Remember, saying no is not saying no to the person; it's saying no to the ask. Pick a few past opportunities that you wish you'd said no to. Compose a concise no for those opportunities that considers how you want to show up, your energy levels, and your priorities.

For example:

Thank you for the lovely offer to teach a three-hour workshop on the craft of poetry. It sounds like a wonderful opportunity. Because I'm currently focusing on [add in priority] and need to conserve my energy, I'll have to decline.

Because the response is concise and connected to your current priorities, you'll feel less guilt for saying no, and you'll feel empowered to reach out to these folks in the future, as will they. If guilt is not something you experience when saying no, this will still help you preserve your energy because you won't find yourself saying yes to things you don't want to do.

Let's dig deeper: Sometimes saying no is a firm and permanent no. But sometimes your no is temporary, meaning it's only a no for this season. When this is the case, you can liken saying no to planting a seed. A seed you can water and come back to next season when the timing and conditions are right to say yes. Last year I was asked to build and teach a series of in-person workshops for an organization whose values aligned beautifully with mine. It would have paid well, too. But it was pretty short notice, and because I now understood how to manage my energy, I knew that I already had too many projects on the go. I knew I wouldn't have the time I needed to build the workshops to my standards and still have the energy to show up and deliver them. I slowed down and assessed the situation:

- Our values aligned! I wanted to work with these folks. I knew this was a place where I could safely have all the conversations I wanted to be having.
- Even though I understood what saying yes would do to my energy, I still felt pressure to accept because it's hard to turn down money when it isn't flowing in steadily. I was so thankful that I had worked on my mindset, because I knew that I would have other opportunities.

- Even though I was booked up, I still wanted to be considered for this workshop opportunity in the future. I knew my no was going to be temporary, so I had to word my response strategically. I had to plant a seed.

Here's that example again, but with a seed planted at the end:

Thank you for the lovely offer to teach a three-hour workshop on the craft of poetry. It sounds like a wonderful opportunity. Because I'm currently focusing on [add in priority] and need to conserve my energy, I'll have to decline, ***but I would love for you to keep me in mind for future opportunities that might better align with my schedule. If you could be in touch at least three months in advance, that would be much appreciated.***

I asked them to keep me in mind for an upcoming season, and I also asked that they give me at least three months' notice to allow me to prepare and show up as my best self. Fun fact: They did come back to me, and with plenty of notice. It ended up being one of my most nourishing projects!

7. BE OPEN TO SAYING YES WITH CONDITIONS

Sometimes you'll want to say yes to an opportunity but there is something stopping you. It might be something small, so instead of saying no, try saying yes with conditions.

For example:

Thank you for your lovely offer to teach a three-hour workshop on the craft of poetry. It sounds like a lovely opportunity. I would love to accept, but only if it were possible to [insert small condition here].

Try a few say no with love responses below. And if you want to take this exercise to the next nerd level, create email templates using these loving nos.

Chelene's Vault

I experienced a brutal burnout in 2017–18. I was a single mom living in low-income housing, with a job that required me to commute for over an hour on public transit. Most of my writing happened on the bus (if I could get a seat) or in the workplace restroom. So, when writing opportunities landed in my inbox, I barely skimmed the emails before enthusiastically hitting reply with a yes. I wasn't thinking about how I would manage my energy, how I wanted to show up that season, or even what my priorities were! The unintended consequence of this haste was finding myself buried under a pile of work that didn't align with my passions. I was saying yes to the wrong things and neglecting to nurture my writing in a way that mattered. I began to feel drained in a way I couldn't quite grasp. Resentment seeped in. I was merely surviving.

I was running myself ragged trying to be so many things for so many people. I stopped sleeping, I only ate when I could be on the move at the same time (I ate a lot of wraps), and I had zero energy to spend with my then fourteen-year-old. I was a single parent, managing editor at a popular magazine, about to promote my second book, working a city job, commuting everywhere on unreliable transit, battling complex familial relationships, getting ready to build out a literary festival... and all with zero boundaries, no energy curation, no intentionality. Add on the factors of oppression of being a Black woman trying to thrive in a cis white male-dominated world, and I was hanging on by a thread. Although I didn't know it back then, it was an incredibly dangerous time for me. I won't lie, it makes me emotional when I look back and picture myself in that state. Even though I got through it, I wasn't experiencing any real joy. I wish that old version of me could see how much control I really had. So, if you take away anything from this journal, let it be that. You have so much control over how you show up for yourself.

LEARN *How to Manage Your Energy*

I am a firm believer that we don't need more time; we need to get better at managing our energy. I'll admit, this opinion does ruffle some feathers, but that's because once you hear the phrase *get better at*, you realize there is work to be done and it is up to you to do it. Being strategic about how I use my energy has transformed my entire life. I feel powerful when I make decisions, when I say no, and when I ask for something outside the box. Promoting my fourth book feels like night and day from book one. I'm not passively waiting for instructions; instead, I'm making moves that feel aligned with who I am as a writer and who I am becoming. What a gift! It took me almost ten years to get to this point, but it doesn't have to take that long for you. You have a wonderful guide!

The narrative throughline for Breathing Space Creative is a focus on energy management for prevention of burnout and burnout recovery, and our Say No with Love Method is at the core of this work. I've watched intentional energy management shapeshift authors' careers. In today's world, we're all pushed to our limits and expected to consistently produce, to give from ourselves without any tangible tools to replenish. Here are eight ways to help you set up a foundation for taking back agency around how you spend your energy.

1. PROTECT YOUR TIME

This is more than just blocking out categorized time in your calendar; in order to truly stick to what you've blocked off, you must create an emotional narrative around why that time deserves to be protected in your calendar. To create an emotional narrative, you have to imagine two things:

1. What would your life look like if you couldn't stick to this time block and you were never able to do this task again?

2. What would your life look like if you stuck to what you prioritized in your calendar?

Look over the fence to see what is possible. Often, we lose momentum or interest because we can't see or dream what life *could* look like. Give yourself a moment to dream. Once you have this time block in your calendar, be sure to make things easy on yourself and add notes and links to documents or folders so that when you see that time block you know exactly what actions to take.

What would your life look like if you couldn't stick to this time block?

___

___

___

___

___

What would your life look like if you stuck to what you prioritized in your calendar?

___

___

___

___

___

2. PROTECT YOUR MORNING ROUTINE

You devoted the time and energy to building this routine, so now you gotta protect it! What you do in the morning will dictate how you use your energy throughout the day. Make sure the first thirty minutes of your day are for you. Jot down your morning routine below and your plans for sticking to it:

3. STOP MAKING YOURSELF SO AVAILABLE

In today's world, the ways in which we communicate have evolved and expanded. It can be incredibly difficult to step away. But you have control over where you show up and how you communicate. Consider how you want to communicate and how you want to make yourself unavailable everywhere else by deleting apps or reducing notifications. Do you really need to be notified that you have an email across four different devices? In the space below, pick up to four ways you want to communicate and map out which ones you will remove your access to.

---

4. CHANGE HOW YOU SPEAK ABOUT YOURSELF AND YOUR WRITING

Retrain your brain! This is where those affirmations come in handy. If we're in a room full of people talking, the loudest voice, the one we hear the clearest, is often our own. List three things that make you the incredible person and writer you are and remind yourself of these daily. Squeeze them into conversations if you can. When you speak positively about yourself and your writing, over time, you will begin to believe that narrative.

1. ______________________________

2. ______________________________

3. ______________________________

5. LIMIT DECISION-MAKING

This is my fave! Prepare for "tomorrow you." Which decisions can you make in advance to protect and conserve as much energy as possible? Small things add up, like preparing your lunch or breakfast in advance, prepping what you plan to wear, or leaving your work bag packed and by the door. Make a list of at least ten things you can do to preserve energy through limiting decision-making.

____

____

____

____

____

____

____

____

____

____

6. PROTECT A "NO MEETING DAY" ONCE PER WEEK

This is the move that changed the game for me. When I was working as a literary agent, I would find myself hopping on calls without notice or preparation because everything felt urgent. I ended up tired because

I had not protected a day that was *just* for client work and a day for moving at my own pace. Having a day where you control how fast or how slow you move will help you have more autonomy over your time. What do you imagine a no-meeting day would look like for you?

---

7. WATCH WHAT YOU CONSUME

What you eat and drink, who you spend your time with, what you watch on TV, what you absorb when scrolling on social media—it all affects your energy. You can control where and when you absorb the news and for how long. You can also curate your social media feed by following people who push out messages that inspire you instead of those that drain you. Write in the space below all the ways in which you might better curate what you consume and why it's important for you.

---

8. CHECK IN WITH THESE INTENTIONS SEASONALLY

Make it easy for yourself—no excuses! This can be as simple as adding a check-in time block in your calendar that repeats every season. I even have a little printable checklist in my Google Drive that I link to right from my calendar.

LEARN *How to Set Realistic Expectations*

Friends, I know you did some big dreaming in chapter 1, but now it's time to come back down to reality for a moment. Looking back at what you jotted down in the **Dream** chapter, what do you think you're capable of taking on right now? Consider what you know to be true about your current patterns (Do you tend to give up quickly when things get hard?), people (Who do you have in your life who can celebrate you?), and projects (What's already on your plate?). What goals do you want to focus on and why?

Goals, goals, goals! This word can be oh so fraught, right? But what if we changed the language? If you feel resistance to language in some way, it's important to ask yourself why. Is there another way I can say this? Adding the word *soft* in front of *goal-setting* changed the way I approached it. Try reframing the phrase *goal-setting* below:

____

Consider three to five______________________ you want to happen because your book exists in the world. Why are these goals important to you?

1. ______________________________________

2. ______________________________________

3. ______________________________________

4. ______________________________________

5. ______________________________________

3 TIPS *For Tracking Your Growth*

Imposter syndrome shows up at the worst times. It creeps in every time I kick off a new project. Those pesky thoughts that whisper, *Who am I to write this?* or *Will anyone even care about my work?* They're like weeds in a creative garden, and they often come from deep within us. But tracking your growth can provide you with a clear and actionable picture of how you're bridging the gap between your current state and where you aspire to be in your creative life. It's important to prioritize the time to track your progress because it not only creates motivation but also boosts your confidence, serving as a constant reminder of your underlying purpose. Looking back isn't always easy, as it may require confronting uncomfortable truths. However, here are three ways to put your growth-tracking skills into action:

1. **Assess your current position.** This is a step we often overlook. Take the time to be present in the moment, observe where you are, and reflect on how it feels to be in this place. Take note of the current beliefs, behaviours, actions, and individuals that have influenced your current situation, both positively and negatively.
2. **Envision where you want to be in the future.** You can revisit the **Dream** chapter and draw inspiration from the ideas you've jotted down there.
3. **Reflect on what you've learned from past experiences.** Be specific about how you will do this. Will you commit to writing in your notebook weekly? Can you prepare a set of general reflection questions in advance?

Chelene's Vault

Impostor syndrome is a real struggle for writers. I even felt like an impostor when I thought about sharing this piece about imposter syndrome with you! Here's what I do to pump up my confidence and level up my creative game: I keep a personal growth tracker. It's an inventory of all the cool stuff I do for myself—taking mindfulness classes, getting mentorship, picking up new skills, and investing in me. The cool part? Every little bit of personal growth has a direct impact on my professional performance. It's like magic. I schedule myself a few minutes weekly to skim through and add to this tracker (the tracker is a simple Google Sheet, by the way). It's a reminder that I'm on this awesome journey of self-improvement and that I'm totally worth it. What I have to offer holds value. It's how I build a new narrative for myself through new behaviours. Think of it as a resumé for your inner self or a CV for the soul, proof that you're committed to getting better and better.

WRITING PROMPT *Explore Growth and Self-Discovery*

Write about a moment in your life when you felt truly alive and in tune with your authentic self. What were you doing, who were you with, and what emotions did you feel? Reflect on what made that moment special and how you can bring more of that authenticity into your daily life. Try to evoke the five senses as you write.

EXERCISE *Let Go of Limiting Beliefs*

In my work with writers and busy professionals, I noticed a common theme: *They were all carrying something they needed to let go of.* Whether it was from past trauma, or mindset issues like not feeling like a good enough writer, or even something a bit more general like not being sure how to prioritize all the stuff they had going on in their life, it was getting in the way of their growth and their happiness, and they wanted to let it go.

WHAT IS LETTING GO?

Think of letting go as removing the training wheels from a bicycle. At first, you might feel scared and uncertain, but as you pedal forward, you discover a newfound sense of balance and freedom. Remember, this isn't about passively letting things go; it's about making space for all the things you *think* you have no time for.

WHAT HAS LETTING GO DONE FOR ME?

Letting go has:

- Allowed me to push myself and build an entire business from scratch.
- Given me the mindset to work on multiple books at once without getting overwhelmed.
- Helped me call in tasks that I had been avoiding my whole life, like driving. (Yes, I learned to drive at forty-two!)
- Helped me reframe some of the most tumultuous relationships in my life.
- Helped me say yes to the right projects, people, and spaces.

Think about all the things you want to let go of then write down one and why it's important to you.

For example:

- A narrative connected to something you have told yourself you could never achieve.
- A past experience that has been haunting you.
- A belief that is harmful to your growth.
- A behaviour that forces you to show up as a different person.

____

____

____

The lifelong process of freeing yourself from limiting beliefs begins with three steps:

1. EXERCISE SELF-COMPASSION BY STARTING YOUR "RELEASE ME" JAR

Starting with a small tangible act of letting go is a wonderful way to acknowledge what you want to let go of. Find a jar or other container where you can start dropping off what you wish to release written on slips of paper (just like you've been doing with the **Mind Dump** [page 15] in this journal!). The Release Me Jar activity offers a heartfelt and hands-on approach to the process of letting go of limiting beliefs. You're not only signalling your commitment to addressing them but also giving that process a place of priority in your life. This simple act is also a beautiful way to track your growth. You can pull your jar out at the end of the year, read each belief, and consider your progress. How much closer are you to really letting that thing go?

2. CALL IN INTENTIONAL COMMUNITY

Who is the best person to help you let go of this limiting belief and why? I used to share everything with anyone who would listen, but I often found myself disappointed or unsatisfied with what I got in return. I had a coach say, "Stop going to the hardware store to shop for milk," and that changed everything for me. I was going to all the wrong places for what I needed. I realized that not everyone is capable of giving me what I need, and that I have to be intentional about who I share things with and what I need in return. Now, when I'm struggling to let go of something, I think about who the best person is to speak to and why. What do I need? What can I give them in return?

Tips for calling in your intentional community:

1. Free-write about what this community could look like for you.
2. Make a list of who you think you can go to for what and why.
3. Think about who you can talk to when you know you need to be championed or reminded of how awesome you are. Be intentional.

3. WORK ON YOURSELF

What areas of your life do you want to grow in? Maybe you want to get better at communication. Maybe you want to learn something you weren't taught when you were young. Whatever it is, call it in and be consistent. Remember, when you consistently work on yourself, letting go becomes a byproduct of the work you've done. Use the space below to jot down some ways you'd like to grow. (Start that personal development tracker, y'all!)

Reflection

Be Kind, but Be Honest

A consistent reflection practice will allow you to track your personal growth, because when you look back at your reflections you will be able to pinpoint what's changed and what you've learned. Spend a few minutes reflecting on how you feel about the materials you worked through in the **Learn** chapter. What surprises you? What excites you? What scares you? Write like no one will ever read this.

CHECK-IN CORNER *Let Go and Keep Safe*

Did anything surprise you in the **Learn** chapter? This is one of the fullest chapters in this journal, so give yourself additional time to work through your experience. Drop some things off in the **Mind Dump** (page 15) if you need to. Is there anything you need to add to your **Inventory** (page 12) or **Safe** (page 10)?

Notes

Love yourself enough to set boundaries. Your time and energy are precious. You get to choose how you use it. You teach people how to treat you by deciding what you will and won't accept.

—Anna Taylor, *Relief*

Chapter 4

Balance

Jumping into the realm of emotions, tackling negative habits, and mastering the art of self-talk can be quite the journey. In this chapter, we'll explore various entry points to help you craft a more balanced work, creative, and life equilibrium.

BALANCE *Intention and Affirmation*

My intention for this chapter is to

The affirmation I will say to myself throughout this chapter to hold up that intention is

BALANCE *Micro Mistakes*

Today's burnout culture is terrifying. The demands of modern life, especially in fast-paced creative industries, can really wear people out. As a writer, editor, and coach, I understand how the pressure to constantly perform and the never-ending to-do lists can be a lot to handle. Take a moment to list some ways burnout has affected your life.

Burnout is often deeply rooted in complex behaviours and systems of oppression, but in this journal, we are all about working on the things we have control over. Over the years, I've found that there are two micro mistakes that lead to big-time burnout: making ourselves overly available and receiving too many notifications across our devices. Here are some ways to balance our availability to avoid burnout.

1. STOP MAKING YOURSELF OVERLY AVAILABLE

Not everyone deserves twenty-four-hour access to you. Brainstorm ways to become *less* available. Start by mapping out all the ways people can get in touch with you, and make a plan to close some of these doors or create boundaries for each method. For example: X message, Instagram message, text, email, phone call, voice mail. How can you remove some of these options? How can you create a boundary around how folks get in touch with you? You can revisit **LEARN How to Manage Your Energy** from the **Learn** chapter (page 84) and take them further here.

2. MANAGE DEVICE NOTIFICATIONS

I was diligently working on a client project at my desk when a thunderstorm of alerts erupted from all my devices—phone, laptop, desktop, iPad—all screaming the same message: *You've got mail.* Not only did this disrupt my creative flow, but it also left me feeling irritated. That was the turning point. The constant barrage of alerts can lead to anxiety and overwhelm. Think of your email inbox as if it were the physical door to your office. Imagine being at your office twenty-four-seven, welcoming anyone and everyone who walks through that door. That's precisely what we're doing with email when we fail to set boundaries. So I took charge of my digital life. I took the radical step of turning off all notifications and instead implemented scheduled email check-in times. Now, I dictate when and where I'm notified, putting me firmly in control.

Assign a purpose to each of your devices. For example: My phone is only for personal use, so I have removed access to email and work alerts *or* my desktop computer is only for work, so this is where I will receive my Slack notifications.

Curate notifications based on devices. For example: You only get Slack notifications on your desktop.

Follow through with the consequences attached to your boundaries. Boundaries are about you, not other people. For example, if you break your "no email to your phone" boundary, what are the consequences?

BALANCE *What You Share about Your Book*

While working on this journal, I was about one month into the promotional period for my previous book, *Let It Go*. Promoting a book while writing another book *about* promoting a book gave me fresh insights to share. It was as though I could look my mistakes in the face and create solutions for future me.

Sharing bits and pieces about the process of writing your book can be a wonderful way to build community, reflect, increase curiosity, and plant seeds for your upcoming launch into the world. But I don't recommend sharing excerpts because details like ideas, plot, and titles can change over time. Instead, share what writing the book is teaching you about yourself. Talk about how you've been balancing the writing with your other obligations. It's the best way to tell people about your book without *really* telling them about your book.

One of my favourite ways to talk about a book-in-progress on social media is to share not only big learnings but also my stumbling blocks. This helps you build trust with your fellow writers and readers. You're also showing your audience that you're human. Fun fact: When you share a stumbling block in the right place, the right people will share ideas to help you overcome that challenge!

Here's an example of a big learning I shared on social media when I was writing my novel, *Junie*:

Writing this book is teaching me that shape and structure matter so much. I feel in control when I can use my poetics to drive my narrative. I'm having fun today just building a world for my character. A world she's always wanted.

A string of comments and questions followed:

- Curiosity: *Oh wow! Tell us how poetry plays a role in your fiction!*
- Building an audience: *Umm, I didn't know you were writing a novel! I can't wait to read it.*
- Building community: *OMG me, too! I thought I was the only one who took so much time with the shape.*

Write some examples of insights you could share about your book in progress:

Why are you sharing? What are you hoping for in return?

Where is the best place to share this? Where are your people and which platform do you enjoy using?

BALANCE *Your Negative Emotions*

In today's pressure-filled, everything-has-a-life-or-death-deadline world, slowing down can be one of the most difficult tasks. When negative feelings arise (maybe in response to feedback about your writing or an opportunity that fell away), it can be difficult to slow down and acknowledge them before responding. But I've come up with a short, simple process for balancing negative emotions.

Jot down a recent time you felt a negative emotion. For example: *I felt rejected when I received an email that my poem had not been selected for publication.*

Now take a deep breath and work through the following ALARTT steps. This process is all about slowing down to figure out how you're feeling and how to respond instead of reacting. It should take you one to three minutes—give it a try!

Acknowledge the feeling—do something tangible like say it out loud or write it down.

Listen to the feeling—what is it telling you about what you need, and how can you deliver on that need?

Ask yourself *why* you feel this way.

Remind yourself of positive affirmations.

Take action—what do you need to do next in order to move on?

Track the length of time you stayed inside the emotion.

---

3 TIPS *For Getting Rid of Unhealthy Habits*

Everything we do, build, believe, and dismantle has to start from the self. The slow investigative work you do in all areas of your life is going to help you call in the creative lifestyle you want. And the more you work on yourself, the more you will start to feel the need to ditch some of the more unhealthy habits, beliefs, and narratives you hold. As you work on balancing your life by prioritizing the things that are the most important to you, unhealthy habits will start to disappear. They won't belong in the life you've started to create for yourself anymore, and you'll be motivated to work on getting rid of them. The slow fade of unhealthy habits then becomes a byproduct of the work you've done.

First, define *unhealthy* for yourself.

____

____

____

____

____

____

Next, list all the unhealthy habits in your life that you want to fall away, such as unfulfilling relationships, eating habits, drinking and smoking, or too much screen time. And, no, listing them here isn't going to make them magically disappear, but it will help you acknowledge them and figure out where to start. To make space for an intentional life as an author, we have to create the conditions for that luscious garden to grow and thrive.

Unhealthy habits I want to eliminate from my life:

____

____

____

____

____

____

____

____

____

____

From the above list, the habit that is causing the most damage is

____

Add the elimination of this unhealthy habit to your **Say No with Love Map** (page 129).

Here are three tips to help you get rid of that unhealthy habit:

1. **Do the adjacent work first.** When you work on becoming a better version of yourself, something magical happens—those unhealthy habits start to stand out like a sore thumb,

practically begging to be dealt with. And your approach to tackling them shifts, too. It's not about avoidance anymore; it's about genuinely wanting to kick those habits to the curb while recognizing that this takes work. You'll realize that the pain of not addressing them is greater than doing the work to alleviate them.

2. **Choose your unhealthy habit wisely.** When you find yourself faced with more than one unhealthy habit, go after the one that's holding you back the most. It's normal for a bunch of negative habits to show up when you're trying to improve as a writer, or just as a person in general. But don't stress yourself out by trying to fix everything at once. Choose the one that feels like the biggest roadblock and start there.

3. **Imagine what your life could be like without this unhealthy habit getting in the way.** It might be hard to picture the other side of the fence, but this exercise is crucial for self-reflection. Personally, it has helped me transform my life. I explore this concept in detail in my book *Let It Go*. By envisioning how I wanted to feel without the burden of toxic relationships, I gradually reframed and even let go of those relationships, all without feeling guilty. It was tough, but it began right here, with the tools in this journal. So take a moment to dream and reflect on what your life could look like without this unhealthy habit holding you back. Fun fact: You'll notice your energy increase. And that extra energy will turn into more creative writing space!

WRITING PROMPT *Explore Emotional Texture*

Write a scene where your character faces a significant obstacle or challenge. If you're working on nonfiction, you can use yourself as the character. Explore the depths of their emotions as they confront this obstacle. What fears, doubts, or insecurities arise within them? How do they summon the courage to push forward despite these emotions? Describe the inner journey your character undergoes as they navigate this obstacle. Do they emerge stronger and more resilient? Show how their emotions evolve throughout the scene, highlighting the transformative power of determination and self-discovery.

EXERCISE *Daily Mindful Breathing*

Each day, find a quiet space for a few minutes. Close your eyes and focus solely on your breath. Take slow, deep breaths, inhaling through your nose and exhaling through your mouth. Pay close attention to the sensation of your breath entering and leaving your body. Let go of any distractions and simply be present with your breath. This daily mindful breathing exercise can help you centre yourself, reduce stress, and find balance in your life while working on your book. I keep a yoga mat and a small cushion beside my desk. It's convenient and it acts as a visual reminder that I have control and I can take a five-minute break if I need one.

Please note that intentional focus on the breath can sometimes be triggering for folks who've experienced post-traumatic stress or have been diagnosed with post-traumatic stress disorder. Always try to adjust these tips and tools to suit you. Taking care of yourself is paramount.

Reflection

Be Kind, but Be Honest

A consistent reflection practice will allow you to track your personal growth, because when you look back at your reflections you will be able to pinpoint what's changed and what you've learned. Spend a few minutes reflecting on how you feel about the materials you worked through in the **Balance** chapter. What excites you? What scares you? Write like no one will ever read this.

CHECK-IN CORNER *Let Go and Keep Safe*

Did anything surprise you in the **Balance** chapter? You can drop it off in the **Mind Dump** (page 15). Are there any resources you need to add to your **Inventory** (page 12) or **Safe** (page 10)?

Notes

First forget inspiration. Habit is more dependable. Habit will sustain you whether you're inspired or not. Habit will help you finish and polish your stories. Inspiration won't. Habit is persistence in practice.
—Octavia E. Butler

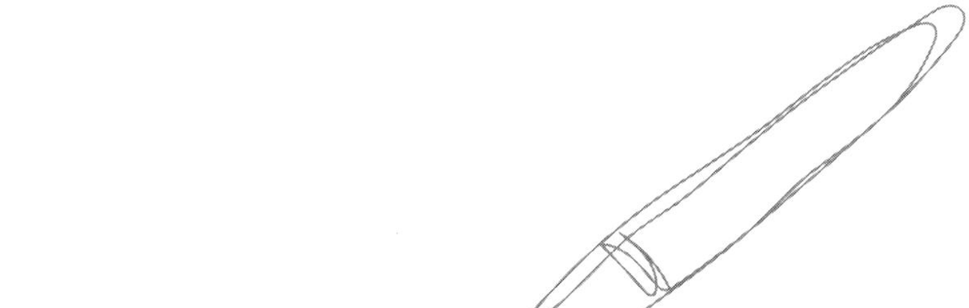

Chapter 5

Create

It's time to put into action a lot of the mindset work you've done. This involves crafting your Say No with Love Map, identifying your non-negotiables, and defining your project pillars. Are you ready to dive in?

CREATE *Intention and Affirmation*

My intention for this chapter is to

The affirmation I will say to myself throughout this chapter to hold up that intention is

CREATE *Your Say No with Love Map*

Remember when you learned **How to Say No with Love** (pages 73–82)? It's now time to create your Say No with Love Map using your notes on how you want to show up, your theme for the year, and your three to five top priorities.

You can use your Say No with Love Map as a filtration system. Each category acts as a filter through which you move an opportunity. You can decide how many of the bullet points need to be met to determine whether you want to say yes or no to the opportunity. Feel free to draw your own map in the space below or create one like I did! (Flip to page 131 for a blank template.)

**The Bigger World:
How do I want to show up?**

- **Be the master of my own experience**
- **Listen to others**
- **Be curious**
- **Challenge beliefs**
- **Push for change**
- **Move with confidence**
- **Laugh**
- **Read, learn, absorb**

Theme/lens/action

**F
L
O
W**

My FALL 2023 Annual Priorities

1. **Get my driver's licence**
    - setting my affirmations before each lesson
    - sticking to my lesson schedule
    - setting a date for the test
    - practising when I have extra pockets of time
2. **Complete first draft of guided journal**
    - protect my weekend writing time
    - make sure I stretch during the week because if my body is sore, I tend to skip my writing
3. **Motivating movement**
    - give myself a theme for each week and an area of focus
    - create a list of fun cardio activities to mix things up
    - what are some indoor cardio routines?
4. **Money mindset WERK**
    - use my expertise to make additional $$
    - continue rejigging my investment goals
5. **Fall craft focus**
    - sign up for courses and workshops that excite!
    - invest in myself
    - as a writer I am a business, too

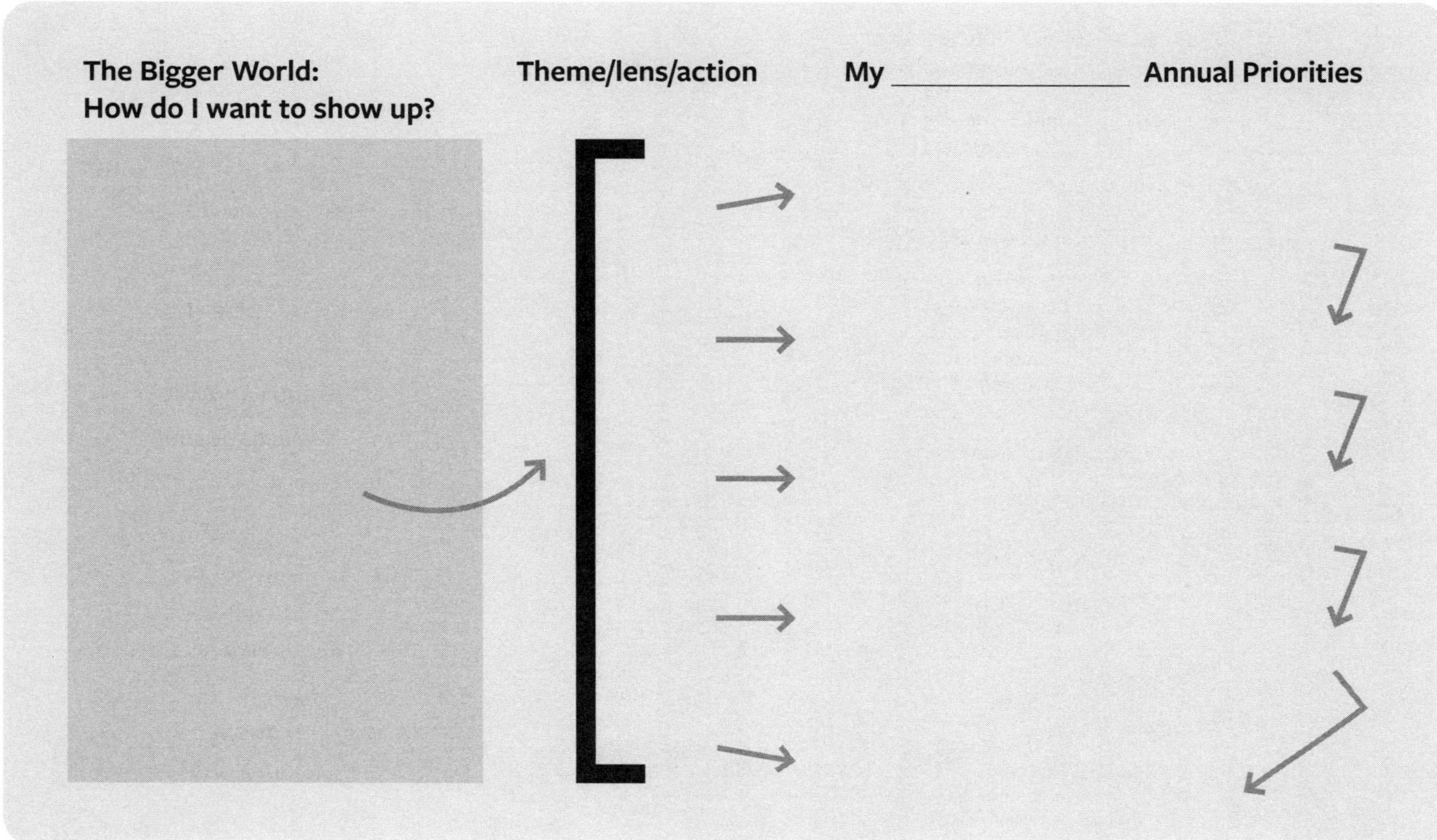
The Bigger World:
How do I want to show up?
Theme/lens/action
My ______________ Annual Priorities

CREATE *Your Book Non-Negotiables*

In one of my early publishing classes, the instructor shared an important lesson about handling feedback and change requests in a book project at the publishing level. Instead of pushing back against every little change, the key was to identify what truly mattered to you and your book and to be able to explain *why* those things were so crucial. This lesson stuck with me and made me want to strengthen this idea of controlling how I showed up in the writing and publishing world. So I developed a straightforward process based on this idea.

This process centres on the concept of non-negotiables. Non-negotiables are about asserting your influence and ensuring you have a significant say in the final outcome of your book project and how the world sees you as a writer. Think of non-negotiables as the essential tasks connected to the broader goal of setting boundaries in your book project. Alongside your why and your book's action, these non-negotiables inform the decisions you make as an author, and each one should have a clear rationale behind it. When creating your non-negotiables, try to widen the lens and look at your values, your personality, your definition of success, and even your message as a writer! How can what you know to be true about who you are flow into what you want for this specific book?

My values

____

____

____

____

My personality

My definition of success (pull your answer from page 26 of the **Dream** chapter)

My message as a writer

Now, let what you've written here inform as many non-negotiables for this book as you can think of.

For example:

I will not change the ending. Even though it is not a happy one, I have given my protagonist agency. It's essential to me that I showcase how complex familial relationships don't always evolve the way we hoped, and I want the women in my books to have a voice.

Select three non-negotiables that you want to prioritize and ask: "Why is this so important?" and "How can I best communicate the importance of this non-negotiable if I have to?"

For example:

This non-negotiable is important to me because, as a Black woman writer, I've been speaking in a variety of spaces about empowering other Black women and I want to continue being a voice for these conversations.

The non-negotiable is rooted in the author's values and a clear why that also connects to her values and how she wants to show up. This, my friends, is the early work of author branding.

1. ______________________________

2. ______________________________

3. ______________________________

CREATE *Your Book Description*

Use the space below to whip up an initial draft of your book description. Consider the intricate themes explored in your book, the distinctive journey your characters embark on (if it's a memoir, you are the character), and the key message you want your readers to take away from your story. Your book description will shapeshift as the book evolves, and your publisher will help, too, but you'll need to have something to start with, so let it be messy! If you're in search of guidance, consider checking out the descriptions for your beloved books. However, keep in mind that this is a golden opportunity for uninhibited creativity!

CREATE *Your Project Pillars*

Making decisions about our writing projects can be difficult, especially if we aren't creating our own intentional processes. Any time you have to make a decision about your book, lean on your project pillars: your why, your book's action, and your book's non-negotiables. Hello, clarity! And the great news is that you've already done most of the work building these pillars. Pool those answers in the space provided below:

Your why (from page 43 of the **Discover** chapter)

Your book's action (from page 47 of the **Discover** chapter)

Your book's non-negotiables (from page 135 of the **Create** chapter)

3 TIPS *For Selecting Your First Readers*

How will you know when to share your work and who to share it with? Here are three tips for how to strategically prepare for feedback for your current draft:

1. KNOW WHERE YOU ARE

Sharing your work and selecting who to share it with depends on where you are with that draft. Are you still visioning? Consider working with someone who is good at planning the shape of a book before anything has been drafted. This is someone who can sort through the trash, find that one thing you shouldn't have thrown away, and then help you brainstorm all the possibilities for the book (this is my specialty!). Have you written a rough first draft? Plan to share your work with someone who understands how to wade through the mess without getting distracted by it. Are you nearing the finish line and the draft is super polished? Work with an editor who can suggest changes to your shape while also looking at your work at the sentence level.

2. UNDERSTAND AND COMMUNICATE THE TYPE OF FEEDBACK YOU NEED

This is the part writers often skip. We thrust our heart work into someone's hands, expecting them to know what to do. If your work is in the first draft stage, chances are copy-editing notes won't be helpful to you. You may still be cutting pages and scenes and chapters. Be clear about what type of feedback you need right now. You can even set your reader up with a few focus questions to make sure their feedback is on track. For example:

- *This is a very raw draft. I'm not ready for copy-editing suggestions at this stage, but could you tell me how you feel as you read? What emotions come up for you?*

- *I've been struggling with building the tension throughout my novel. Could you focus your feedback in this area?*
- *I'm not sure if my readers will be confused because the point of view jumps around. Can you tell me if this is distracting, and if so, I'd love suggestions for change.*

3. DON'T GO TO THE HARDWARE STORE FOR MILK

How often have we handed over our manuscript to a family member or friend, eager for them to read it, only to receive a nice pat on the head and a "This is great!" There's no way the first draft is great, by the way. Unless your family member or friend is also a writer, they won't understand the writing process, and their feedback won't be helpful to you at this early stage. Your family and friends want to support you, but they might not be able to give objective feedback. Non-writers are not capable of giving you substantive feedback on an early draft. Just like we discussed calling in your circle when it comes to letting go of limiting beliefs, you have to be intentional about deciding who reads your work to make sure you can get what you need. Find the right people for the right stage of your manuscript. For early drafts, try to find readers who understand the writing process and can get past the mess in order to help you develop your ideas. And for polished drafts, try to find readers who have a keen eye for grammar and all things micro! Fun fact: I'm no copy-editor, so I always need help in this area! I often let go of control in this phase and let the pros guide me.

WRITING PROMPT *Write a Letter to an Author You Admire*

A great way to combat unhealthy peer comparison is to write a letter to an author you admire. You can include what you love about their writing, share your own writerly ideas and dreams, and ask burning questions. This is also a great way to lean into gratitude instead of jealousy. You won't be sending this letter, but going through the process can create positive feelings and help you feel more connected to your own unique writing journey.

EXERCISE *Build Your Formula for Incorporating Feedback*

A formula for incorporating or disregarding writerly feedback has been one of the greatest tools I've ever gifted myself. It can be overwhelming to receive feedback, especially from multiple sources. Not knowing what to do with the feedback—or worse, incorporating suggestions that don't feel right for you or the project—can put you in a tough spot creatively.

Here are five steps you can take to build a solid and intentional plan for incorporating feedback:

1. **Plan for your own self-care.** Navigating feedback and deciding which suggestions to embrace and which to let go of can be mentally taxing. It's essential to prioritize self-care during this process and incorporate it proactively into your revision routine. For me, self-care looks like taking frequent breaks, enjoying leisurely walks, and cherishing quality time with my dog, Chester. However, a crucial aspect of my self-care strategy is having a well-structured plan in place. Knowing I have that plan makes me feel good about the work ahead of me. For each book I work on, I create a broad revision checklist that I continue to refine as I receive feedback from early readers or editors. This checklist serves as a guide, providing me with a clear endpoint for each revision stage and the confidence to gracefully transition into the next draft with care.
2. **Set up your space.** Make sure you are in a calm environment when revising.
3. **Acknowledge** how you feel about the feedback and why. Journal about it.

4. **Tuck everything away.** Give the feedback the breathing space it needs. How long you tuck the feedback away is up to you. The point is to come back to it after you've had time to think.

5. **Come back to the feedback with your project pillars.** Use your why, your book's action, and your book non-negotiables to reassess, make decisions, and have a healthy dialogue with your early readers or any editors you might work with at various stages in your process.

My feedback formula is on the next page.

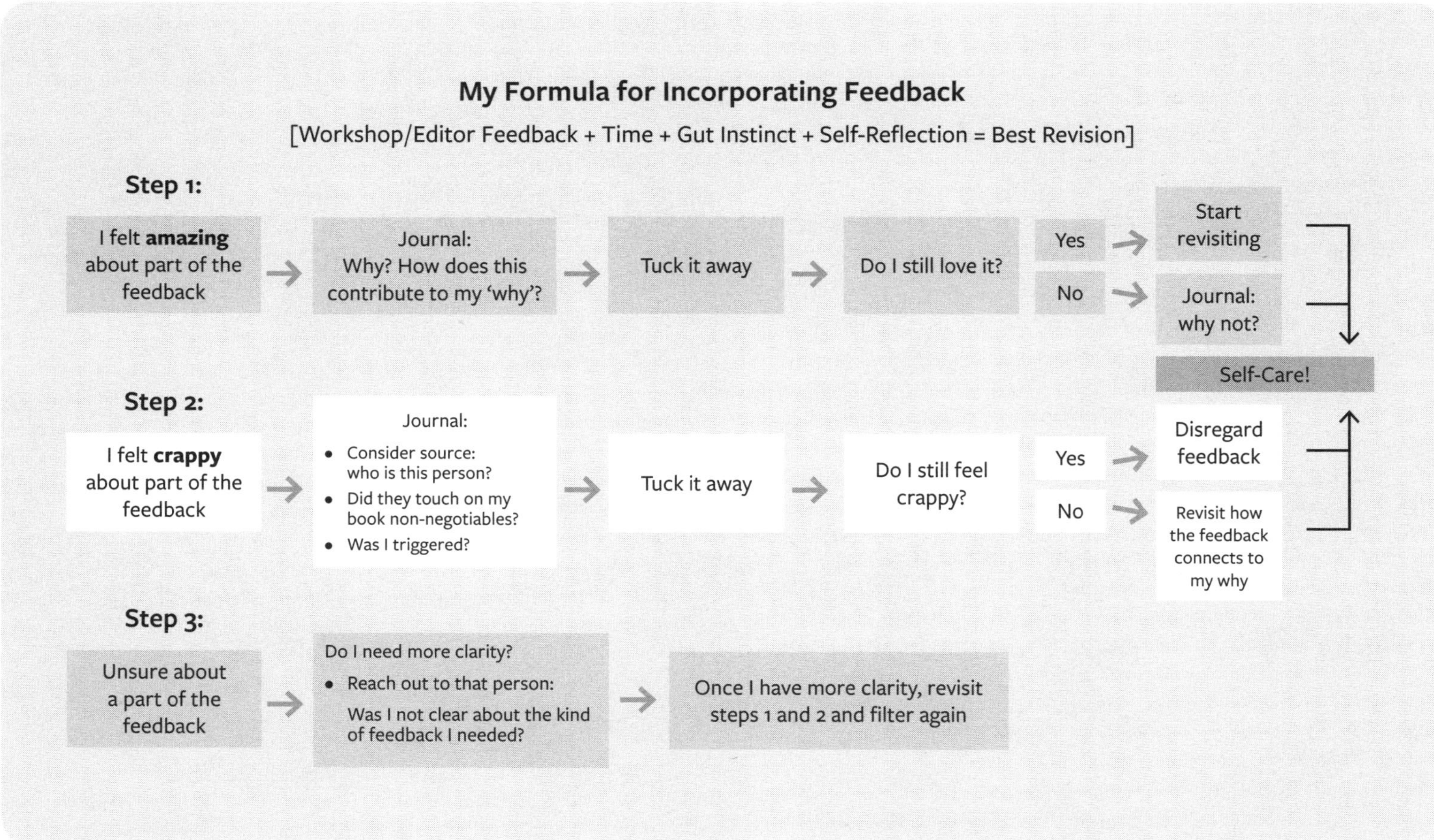
My Formula for Incorporating Feedback
[Workshop/Editor Feedback + Time + Gut Instinct + Self-Reflection = Best Revision]
Step 1:
I felt **amazing** about part of the feedback
Journal: Why? How does this contribute to my 'why'?
Tuck it away
Do I still love it?
Yes
Start revisiting
No
Journal: why not?
Self-Care!
Step 2:
I felt **crappy** about part of the feedback
Journal:
Consider source: who is this person?
Did they touch on my book non-negotiables?
Was I triggered?
Tuck it away
Do I still feel crappy?
Yes
Disregard feedback
No
Revisit how the feedback connects to my why
Step 3:
Unsure about a part of the feedback
Do I need more clarity?
Reach out to that person:
Was I not clear about the kind of feedback I needed?
Once I have more clarity, revisit steps 1 and 2 and filter again

Reflection

Be Kind, but Be Honest

A consistent reflection practice will allow you to track your personal growth, because when you look back at your reflections you will be able to pinpoint what's changed and what you've learned. Spend a few minutes reflecting on how you feel about the materials you worked through in the **Create** chapter. What surprises you? What excites you? What scares you? Write like no one will ever read this.

CHECK-IN CORNER *Let Go and Keep Safe*

Did anything surprise you in the **Create** chapter? You can drop it off in the **Mind Dump** (page 15). Is there anything you need to add to your **Inventory** (page 12) or **Safe** (page 10)?

Part 2

Publishing

The most important part of any plan is to plan on the plan not going according to plan. —Morgan Housel, *The Psychology of Money*

Chapter 6

Prepare

Time to channel your inner entrepreneur! In this chapter, you'll figure out how to treat your writing like a business. How can you make money and build a foundation for a solid creative career?

PREPARE *Intention and Affirmation*

My intention for this chapter is to

The affirmation I will say to myself throughout this chapter to hold up that intention is

PREPARE *Your Definition of Safety*

Any time I've been part of conversations about author branding, folks seemed to overcomplicate it, overlooking the personal elements that enable us to show up as our authentic selves. When you break it down, author branding is all about creating a strategic and intentional approach to how we present ourselves as authors, and the concept of safety plays a pivotal role in this process. As I continue my journey of writing and eventually promoting my fifth book, I've gained valuable insights into what makes me feel comfortable and confident. It's become evident that I feel safe and thrive in environments where I'm encouraged to explore my unique skills, confront my fears, and share my opinions openly.

What does safety look and feel like to you?

Think about how you feel in certain spaces, such as universities or informal talks at literary festivals, and ask yourself what information you need to know about your audience, the event organizer, and the location. Brainstorm questions to ask to feel safe at events:

____

____

____

____

____

____

____

____

Chelene's Vault

Safety to me can feel like a desire to be myself and to let my guard down. I remember feeling extremely safe during an intimate live conversation about my novel, *Junie*. The moderator not only posed thoughtful questions but also took the initiative to schedule a separate meeting with me prior to the event. This meeting was dedicated to discussing how to create an environment that would allow me to bring my best self forward. Looking back, I realize how much more confidently I presented myself during that event compared to others, and it has since played a significant role in shaping my definition of safety.

PREPARE *Your Circle*

We are a direct reflection of the people we spend the most time with, so be intentional about who you call into your writerly world. You want folks in your corner who can support you, celebrate with you, and troubleshoot with you. The folks who can support you and celebrate with you understand your why intimately. They know why you write and will do what they can to make sure you stay inspired. The people who can troubleshoot with you understand the writing process. Remember, you can't shop for milk at the hardware store (page 140)! Make sure the folks you choose for your circle are capable of giving you what you need.

I've learned a great deal about people by paying close attention to how they respond to collaboration outreach. Whether by email, phone, virtual call, or in person, my deep listening skills (remember to call in your superpower!) allow me to pay attention to all the things others may skip or not even notice. Perhaps you've decided that you'd like to collaborate with someone in your field in a unique and innovative manner. Summoning the courage, you compose and send that email or make that phone call. Here are the three most common responses:

1. Genuine curiosity (can see the possibilities and is open to exploring them): *Tell me more!*
2. Disbelief (then leaning in with curiosity to find flaws or debunk): *Impossible. How can that be? How can you be in a position to work on this project?*
3. The brush-off (fear of competition): *I do the same work.*

But what is at the core of these responses? What makes people respond the way they do? What experiences or beliefs have influenced their responses? These are the questions I ask myself instead of taking it personally or writing off the experience. Spend some time building your circles. Keep in mind that some people might overlap and qualify for multiple categories.

Who would you include and why?

Support Circle

Celebration Circle

Troubleshooting Circle

Chelene's Vault

Reaching out to build my circle wasn't always easy for me. I'd been told my whole life that my introverted personality was a negative thing. But I've let go of that limiting narrative and flipped it into my superpower! Through focused coaching and mindfulness, I've learned to see beyond the surface and really understand people. It's all about being present, asking questions instead of giving immediate advice, and realizing that there's often more to their story. My everyday interactions shape how I coach, helping me dig deep to uncover what's truly holding people back, beyond their surface issues. Building a circle of the right people in our lives can be tough, and letting go of the wrong ones is even harder. But building intentional communities doesn't have to be a struggle if you slow down and pay attention to how people respond to you and call on your superpower.

PREPARE *The Entrepreneurial Writer*

Being an author is a business. It's one thing to consider the direct correlation between your book and making money (advances and royalties), but how does having your book in the world become a catalyst for writing-adjacent financial opportunities? If you want to build your writing career strategically, and if you're open to all the various ways in which having a book in the world can help you make a living, you have to make good decisions (thank goodness you have that **Say No with Love Map**, eh?). The decisions you make as a writer will affect your author brand (how you show up, the public-facing you), and your author brand will affect how much money you make.

But first, we should take a short detour to talk about book advances, because how much authors get paid is one of the biggest secrets in the publishing industry. Your book advance depends on many factors, such as:

- The size of the press and whether it's a multinational corporate publisher or an independent press. They have different resources and very different mandates.
- Whether you have an agent to negotiate for you. But they can only do so much! Have realistic expectations.
- Your genre (fiction, nonfiction, traditional, hybrid).
- The marketplace—what people are buying (this bothers me, but it's true).
- The sales from your last book, if applicable. How much does the publishing house sales department think you can sell based on this number? Be sure to communicate how resourceful you are and share a list of connections to communities you have access to, even if you think they're not connected to your book.

- Your brand. In my opinion, this is the factor that matters most to publishers, though I don't really see folks admitting this!

Your book advance is not a one-time payment upfront; it might be broken up into chunks and spread out over a number of years (good luck surviving on that...unless you're a big commercial writer, but most writers do not fall into that category). So how can writers look at their advance as extra and focus their efforts on how their book can create well-paying opportunities that connect to who they are and the messages they want to push out into the world? By considering their author brand.

Because there's a lot in the publishing industry writers can't control, let's look at what you *can* control. You can alleviate a lot of stress and burnout by thinking about your brand early and taking back control over how you show up. Even though your publisher might be able to help you with this, building your author career is *your* job and it's the publisher's job to focus on the book. I've heard plenty of people in the industry push back against this and say this pressure to promote should not be put on authors, but I say, oh yes, it should! I mean, think about it. When it comes to your books, what you speak about, and what messages you push out there, would you really want someone else crafting that for you? No way!

Over time, you'll begin to see the value in having your specific book in the world. A value built not on your advance or royalty payments but on what you've turned them into. And once you find this for yourself, you'll want to keep it safe.

Write a list of the themes in your book that connect to your values and the messages you want to push out into the world.

Write a list of all the writing-adjacent work you would love to call in (speaking gigs, teaching, grant assessing, workshop facilitation, etc.).

How will these projects bring in steady income? Don't worry if you write generally here. You'll have an opportunity to expand on these ideas later.

Where do you need to show up (or who do you need to speak to) to get into these spaces?

Revisit the **Your Circle** exercise from page 155. Who can help you get your foot in the door?

How will these projects encourage personal and professional growth? For example, my books have led me to work with writers in many ways, which then branched out into wider coaching. This led me to certification in mindfulness facilitation, communication, cognitive behavioural therapy, and coaching.

Grants

Hot tip for Canadian writers: Include applying for various grants as a permanent line item in your budget. Even if you're not working on a new project every year, you can apply for various professional development grants to work with mentors, editors, and other creative professionals who can help you expand your writerly toolkit. Check out the Canada Council for the Arts and your provincial and local arts councils for starters. A grant can offer more than just a monetary boost. It can increase your confidence and help you continue to reach for your writing dreams. Need more help? I have a free guide to Canadian grants on my website: cheleneknight.com.

PREPARE *Your Money: Planning, Tracking, and Bill Collecting*

Money can be a complex topic for many (I know it is for me!). The mindset needed to change the negative emotional relationship you have built up with money can be deep and lifelong.

What is your current relationship like with money?

What will you need to change about this relationship with money?

Who in your circle can help you?

____

____

____

____

____

Establish your rates for writing-adjacent work, with a plan to increase your rates as you invest in yourself personally, professionally, and emotionally. Establishing these rates can be challenging. I advise against establishing an hourly rate. Why? Because as you grow, become more efficient, and develop processes, it will take you less time to complete projects, and when you have an hourly rate, you penalize yourself for being efficient. Instead, place a value on the outcome of your work.

For example, if you're delivering a workshop, what outcome will the participants experience? Hot tip: If you're offering a workshop, think about the time and energy it takes to *build* the workshop and *deliver* the workshop. It's smart to have two separate fees, and then later, when the workshop is built, you can simply charge the fee to deliver it. I learned that one the hard way!

If you don't already track your writerly income, now is the time to start. Start simply and move slowly. Find an accounting system that makes sense for you, such as a spreadsheet, a notebook, or a specialized computer program. I use Trello, QuickBooks, and Google Sheets. I have a business chequing account, which I keep separate from my personal accounts. I have another account that is just for taxes. I set aside 30 percent from *all* writing/business-related income for taxes. Anytime I take on a paid gig, I create an invoice in QuickBooks. If the organization requires an invoice, I send one, or I keep it for my records because all income needs to be matched with an invoice. This is called reconciling your transactions. To make sure this reconciliation doesn't pile up on me, I have a recurring task reminder that pops up once a week in my task manager app that prompts me to look at all the invoices in QuickBooks to make sure they have a matching payment. Once you have your process down, you may want to create more complexity; for example, I now have quarterly financial benchmarks.

Establish your accounts: Where will your money go and how will you track money owed to you?

If there are outstanding invoices, I have to put on my bill-collecting hat, which can feel intimidating. But just like you did with your say no with love language, you'll want to build your bill collection language for reaching out about money owed to you. If you need to create a bit of distance, you can create a separate "payments" email sent from another account. I did this for a while before I was able to hire an assistant. Because I often had personal or close relationships with the people and organizations who were hiring me, creating a separate email helped me feel the emotional separation I needed in order to stay on top of my finances.

Here's an example of what my *old* bill collecting language looked like:

From: chelene@cheleneknight.com
To: Organization Name
Subject: Sorry!!! Just checking in about my last event :)

Dear [Name],

I feel so bad bothering you...I just wanted to check in about my event payment? I haven't received it yet and not that it's an issue at all, I just wanted to make sure I didn't miss an email confirming payment? I mean, I'm sure you folks are organized, I just wanted to check in.
Sorry to be a pain :)

Sincerely,
Chelene

Now here's my refined language:

From: payments@cheleneknight.com
To: Organization Name
Subject: Re: Invoice 6281

Dear [Name],

I am writing to follow up on an amount owing [invoice 6281], which is now overdue.

We would appreciate your prompt payment [reiterate payment method options].

If you have any questions, please don't hesitate to contact us.

Sincerely,
Payments CheleneKnight.com

I keep it short, to the point, and don't apologize for reaching out. Now, you give your bill collection language a try!

PREPARE *For the Unexpected*

Part of the joy of being a writer is the excitement of the unknown. Even though the unexpected can also cause anxiety, there's something special about not knowing what's right around the corner. I love dreaming about all the possibilities! How can you shift your focus from anxiety to excitement and gratitude? On the next page is a list of unexpected events that can occur when you publish your book—the good, the bad, and the ugly. Circle the ones that excite you, and circle in another colour the things that scare you. Now, brainstorm how you will handle each instance. You can add more to the list, too!

Event	What makes me anxious about this?	How can I lean into gratitude in this situation?	How will I handle this?
Your book wins an award.			
You get to travel for your book.			
You are a finalist for an award and so is a friend. You win.			
You are a finalist for an award and so is a friend. You lose.			
Your book doesn't seem to be getting much attention.			
You are challenged about the content of your book on stage.			
You are asked questions about your book that you don't know how to answer.			
You receive a negative book review.			
You encounter mean comments online about your book. (I never read the comments anymore, by the way!)			

PREPARE *And Mark Up Your Author Copy*

Your author copy of your book can be a wonderful tool for promoting your book! One of my favourite things to do when I receive my author copy is take out my pens, highlighters, and sticky tabs and begin highlighting sections I like to read from and writing context in the margins. Marking up your book can create ease and streamline decision-making, for example, by pre-determining the sections you will read depending on the space you're in. When I'm in a more personal, informal setting, I might want to read from the sections of my book that are more emotional because I know I'm in a safe space. This kind of intentionality puts you in control. You can select what to share based on reading the room. You have control over how you show up.

What's important to you when it comes to selecting passages from your book to share with your readers? How can you use the work you did in the **Create** chapter to build your non-negotiables (pages 132–35) to inform what you decide to read and talk about?

PREPARE *Your Three Anchors*

Speaking about your book can bring on uncertainty, especially if you're asked a question that makes you uncomfortable or derails the conversation. How will you reply? You have to prepare in advance. You can fall back on your three anchors to navigate difficult questions about your book and steer the conversation back to the topics that are important to you:

1. Your book's unique superpower when it comes to craft and structure.
2. Your book's major themes as they relate to the question.
3. Combine the first two anchors and discuss what this means for the reader's experience.

What are some questions that you anticipate being asked about your book?

For example: *Your novel has a neglectful mother character. Was this based on your own mother?*

Anchor 1: Write a sentence describing your book's unique superpower when it comes to craft and structure.

For example: *My book uses immersive vignettes that are sprinkled throughout the main narrative.*

____

____

Anchor 2: Write a sentence naming one of your book's major themes connected to the question.

For example: *My book focuses on the overarching theme of complex mother-daughter relationships.*

____

____

Anchor 3: Combine the first two anchors and write about what this means for the reader experience.

For example: *That's a very interesting question. My book's unique yet immersive vignettes zero in on the mother character through the deterioration of the world the characters inhabit. This is deeply rooted in the overarching theme of complex mother-daughter relationships. And it was my hope that all mothers would see part of themselves in this character.*

____

____

____

With a reply grounded in your three anchors, you can steer the conversation away from the personal question while distilling the very essence of your book into just a few lines. And this response can then act as a catalyst for a deeper conversation about the book. Finally, you will feel more in control and confident.

PREPARE *The Questions You Want to Be Asked*

When you're promoting your books at events like panels, festivals, or interviews with the media, you might find yourself in the hands of a moderator. But remember what Alice Walker once said, "The most common way people give up their power is by thinking they don't have any." So, let's not give up our power!

You can prepare for this situation by having a list of questions in your back pocket. These are questions that you've thought about beforehand that can guide you into the conversations you *want* to have about your book (oh, hello, author branding!). You can bring up these questions and themes naturally during the conversation, or when the moderator or interviewer asks if there's anything else you'd like to talk about.

For example, I would love to talk about:

- *My process for writing this book.*
- *What I learned about myself through writing this book.*
- *The power of giving agency to my female characters.*

Brainstorm a few questions for yourself in the space below. Think about developing your author brand. What messages do you have for the world? What do you want the world to know about not just this specific book but also who you are as a writer?

3 TIPS *For Dreaming and Planning Your Book Launch*

Just like everything else we've covered so far, it's important to start dreaming about and preparing for your book launch early. You might have to plan your own official book launch. Your publisher will help and support you, but the details will be up to you. And, folks, this can be a good thing! Your book launch is more than just a way to introduce your book to the world; it's an opportunity for growth and connection, to gather your community and celebrate your literary creation in a style that's all you. This means you can put your own stamp on it—you can let your creativity fly. You can truly launch your book with love.

For my first book, I pretty much followed the crowd. I went with a venue that was recommended without really thinking about what I truly wanted. When book number two came around, I put more thought into it, but emotionally, I was unprepared, and it took me a while to bounce back. Book three's launch? Well, I decided to skip it altogether, and honestly, I regret that choice today. But then for book four I went all in, and let me tell you, it was a game-changer for me as a writer.

Here are three tips for organizing your own book launch:

1. BE HONEST WITH YOURSELF ABOUT YOUR LAUNCH

INTENTIONS

- Define what a successful launch means for you.
- Develop a budget. Your publisher may be able to cover a portion of the cost, but be ready to chip in. If you plan intentionally, your book launch will be a worthwhile investment in yourself.
- Create a mini marketing plan to get the word out about the launch (promo for the promo!). Your publisher can help you, but ask your community for help, too. Remember, people want to support you and your book. I had an author friend email me

and others asking us to be a part of her "book launch support squad," and she gave us all tangible yet doable tasks that we could do to support her. I loved her creativity!

- Ask friends, author acquaintances, and others in the community for help with logistics, such as selecting a venue, sending out invites, and managing the event.
- Consider what you want your role to look like. For example, for book four's launch, I had a friend help plan all the details based on a brief I wrote for her so that I could just show up and be present.

2. PLAN THE VIBE

- How do you want your launch to feel? The vibe will influence every other decision you make about your launch, from the venue to the flow of the event to the outcomes.
- Make sure the vibe aligns with your personality and how you want to introduce your book to the world. For example: Do you want to host a big crowd, or do you want to create an intimate living-room feel? Do you want to have a traditional reading with a Q&A? Or do you want to do something totally different?
- What small yet powerful activities do you want to include? At my book launch for *Let It Go*, I set up a ballot box at the front door where folks were encouraged to "let something go." The contents of that box later became a special keepsake for me.
- Consider curating a playlist from the music you listened to while writing the book.

3. DECIDE ON THE FLOW

- Do you plan to have a host? What personality would best suit the intended vibe and launch goal?
- Do you want to have a reading component and then a Q&A? You have full autonomy, so have fun with the structure and think about what you know to be true about you.
- How long do you want the event to be? Consider your energy levels and your boundaries. As someone whose social battery depletes easily, I kept my last book launch to ninety minutes and had a debrief activity planned for afterward with my partner. I also communicated this to the event host so that she could help me exit with grace instead of being pulled into more social invites.

What will your book celebration look like?

Chelene's Vault

It took me four books to figure out the approach to book launches I'm now sharing in this journal. The fantastic launch party for my previous book was a blast. To be honest, this celebration was a long time coming. It brought together exactly the kind of people I wanted to be there. We set the vibe just the way I'd always imagined, with a fun interactive activity right at the front door. Instead of the usual reading, we dove into intimate conversations, which was a fabulous way to highlight my superpower. Oh, and let's not forget the goodie bags I put together for my guests—a little extra touch to show my gratitude and promote local businesses (always thinking about what message I want to push out there). The goodie bags also included my own business swag (because, hello, strategic branding skills!). It was the most awesome event of my career. It was...me.

WRITING PROMPT *Explore a Nervous Character*

Think about a character who's seriously jittery about something important that's about to happen. Describe the situation and get inside their head. What's going on in their mind? How's their body reacting? Show how this nervousness affects their choices, actions, and interactions with others. Do they have any tricks up their sleeve to deal with the jitters? Do they eventually conquer their nerves, or do they ride them out? How does the character feel afterward? How do they lean into the idea of accomplishment? Look over what you've written. Where do you see yourself?

EXERCISE *Get Organized and Build a Process*

When I think about how I've been able to write and promote multiple books at once, teach, run my business, and take care of my family—all without experiencing another burnout—there were two big contributors:

1. Curating exactly how I wanted to show up and managing my energy through setting boundaries and saying no with love.

1. Building as many processes as possible. A process is made up of **workflows** (the steps needed to complete a task), **systems** (the resources used to deliver on those steps), and **automations** (the ways those steps happen more efficiently).

No one is born organized. It's a learned skill. And once you experience how processes can totally transform your day-to-day life, you'll be looking for tasks to build processes around!

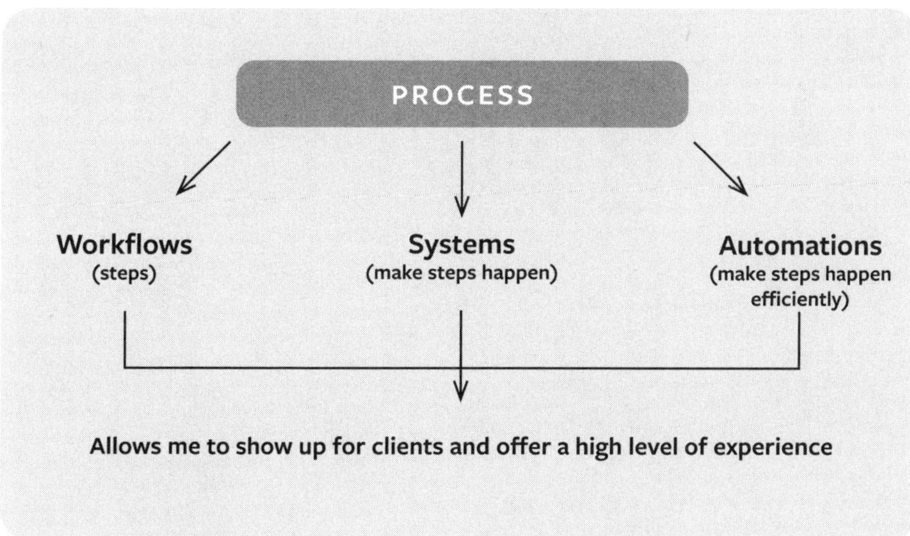

What processes can you build around your writing and publishing tasks? Remember, the more you can automate, the more energy you preserve. I use an app called Trello to map out everything connected to my books. Pick one aspect of your writerly activities that you want to build a clear process for. For example, let's create a process broken down into workflows, systems, and automations for addressing event invites:

WORKFLOW

Steps for considering the invite:

- Remember, your **Say No with Love Map** (page 129) can help you make a decision. Define the basic information you need about the event before you can consider. For example:
    - What are the values of the organization?
    - How much will I be paid?
    - What is the scope of the project, i.e., how much of my time and energy will be required?
    - What will the audience be like?
    - What sort of venue will the event take place in?

Steps for responding to the invite:

- Create a few standard email templates that you can revise and edit as needed. This is especially helpful for declines.

Steps for preparing for the event:

- Create an event prep list—a list of tangible items you will need to bring/have ready.

- Do you need to read/research/prepare a presentation? Remember, knowing the scope of the event is important not only for preparation but also for determining whether you want to take it on at all.

Steps for debriefing post-event:

- Reflect on the event. How does it contribute to your definition of success for this book?
- Do you want to work with this organization again? Add them to your potential future collaborations list.
- Did you deliver a workshop? Did you enjoy it? Would you want to deliver it again? If yes, add it to a workshop folder and schedule yourself to revise/refine the workshop seasonally or annually to keep it relevant. Now, you can pitch yourself to other organizations and your workshop will be ready to go. If your workshop topic is connected to the themes in your book, this is another way to give your book a long shelf life.

SYSTEMS

- Email: to store templates
- Google Docs or Trello: to store the event prep list

AUTOMATIONS

- Calendly: to automate booking/showcase availability for events

My Best Self

I like to surpass expectations and inspire people when I say yes to delivering a keynote or a talk. I want folks to walk away nourished and energized. To do that, I need to know what's expected of me and all the tidbits of information that would help me prepare to show up as my best self. You'd be amazed how many times I have been invited to an event with no details provided aside from the date and time. How can you make an informed decision if you don't know what you're making a decision about? And, yes, the writing and publishing industries can rush you and expect you to say yes to everything. But don't give in! Slow down.

Use the space below to map out your own process made up of workflows, systems, and automations.

Reflection

Be Kind, but Be Honest

A consistent reflection practice will allow you to track your personal growth, because when you look back at your reflections you will be able to pinpoint what's changed and what you've learned. Spend a few minutes reflecting on how you feel about the materials you worked through in the **Prepare** chapter. What surprises you? What excites you? What scares you? Write like no one will ever read this.

CHECK-IN CORNER *Let Go and Keep Safe*

Did anything surprise you in the **Prepare** chapter? You can drop it off in the **Mind Dump** (page 15). Is there anything you need to add to your **Inventory** (page 12) or **Safe** (page 10)?

Publishing a book is like stuffing a note into a bottle and hurling it into the sea. Some bottles drown, some come safe to land, where the notes are read and then possibly cherished, or else misinterpreted, or else understood all too well by those who hate the message. You never know who your readers might be.

—Margaret Atwood

Chapter 7

Publish

Even if your ultimate aim might not be to publish your book, it's still valuable to approach this chapter with curiosity. You'll gain clarity around the distinction between personal branding and marketing, along with some valuable tips to enhance your enjoyment of the production process.

PUBLISH *Intention and Affirmation*

My intention for this chapter is to

The affirmation I will say to myself throughout this chapter to hold up that intention is

PUBLISH *Branding vs. Marketing*

An author brand is all about how you show up. It's all about how you present yourself. It's kind of funny, but I didn't initially realize that what I was teaching authors was directly tied to branding. I thought I was just helping authors take better care of themselves! Marketing, however, is *not* branding. Marketing is necessary to an author brand, like the turbo boost for your branding journey. It's a short-term strategy aimed at making you and your message more visible. Marketing is like the engine in the car. The car is you.

Here are some ways I have used marketing to build my author brand:

- I started a blog dedicated to the themes I talked about in my last book, and I connected these themes to my overall message and values. I might not keep this blog up forever, but during the promo period for my book it will help strengthen my message.
- I built a few workshops and talks that speak to my core message and promoted them during my book promo period. Fun fact: These are workshops I can deliver over and over, which is a fabulous way to increase income, build an audience, and keep a book alive. Take it a step further and offer these workshops in front of someone else's audience. For example, I'll be presenting a workshop in front of an American brand strategist's audience called *Energy Is Currency: 8 Ways to Cultivate a More Sustainable Writing Career*, which pulls from the themes in this journal.
- I created Instagram posts that connected readers to my book *and* the items above.
- I pitched myself for conferences and podcasts *outside* the writing and publishing industry that focus on the themes and messages I want to have conversations about to put me in front of different but aligned audiences.

- I partnered with geographically diverse authors who have similar messages so that we could help each other expand our reach. To do this, I started building relationships over time, knowing that I was planting seeds. These relationships don't just happen overnight!

Use the space below to brainstorm how you might market your book to build your author brand in alignment with your core values, boundaries, and personality.

PUBLISH *Enjoying the Production Process*

Publishing a book is work for everyone involved, but that doesn't mean it can't be a joyful experience. My production experiences were very different with each of my books, but each one informed the next one. In traditional publishing, there are different stages. For each one, think of one to three questions for your publisher, along with one to three exciting outcomes.

MANUSCRIPT SUBMISSION

This is when you submit your manuscript to a publisher according to their guidelines. Some authors have an agent who does this on their behalf. What questions do you have about submitting your manuscript? Consider your circle. Who might be able to help you answer these questions?

1. ______________________________

2. ______________________________

3. ______________________________

Can you predict some exciting outcomes?

1. ______________________________

2. ______________________________

3. ______________________________

CONTRACT SIGNING AND AUTHOR ONBOARDING

Signing your book contract can be daunting. Who can help you determine what questions to ask? If you don't have an agent to help you, you may want to consider your circle. What questions do you have about signing a contract and what will it be like to work with this publisher? Revisit your **non-negotiables** (page 135).

1. ____

2. ____

3. ____

What could be some exciting outcomes?

1. ____

2. ____

3. ____

EDITING AND REVISION

Even though you may think your book is polished and ready to go, once you've signed your contract, your manuscript will undergo yet another series of edits.

1. **Substantive editing.** Substantive editing involves big-picture and structural changes to your book. Think shape. This might include things like the order of scenes, deleting scenes, and adding new ones. Think of a bird flying over your house and taking in all the big details. You can see so much more because you're looking at it all at once.

Questions

1. ______________________________

2. ______________________________

3. ______________________________

Exciting outcomes

1. ______________________________

2. ______________________________

3. ______________________________

2. **Copy-editing.** Copy-editing is a specialized skill and you'll probably have a different editor take on this task. Copy-editing includes grammatical suggestions and some line editing. Copy-editors help your message become clear and your work shine! I love, respect, and adore copy-editors because this is not my area of expertise.

Questions

1. ______________________________

2. ______________________________

3. ______________________________

Exciting outcomes

1. ______________________________

2. ______________________________

3. ______________________________

3. **Proofreading.** The proofreader will review the designed pages of your book for any last mistakes before the book goes to the printer.

   Questions

   1. ______________________________

   2. ______________________________

   3. ______________________________

   Exciting outcomes

   1. ______________________________

   2. ______________________________

   3. ______________________________

COVER DESIGN AND LAYOUT

Cover design usually happens around six months ahead of publication. Design of the book's interior usually happens after copy-editing. This can be a really fun time for the writer, especially if you're working with a publisher who includes their author in the design process. Fun fact:

This doesn't always happen, so if design input and consultation are important to you, ask about the possibility early on.

Questions

1. ______________________________

2. ______________________________

3. ______________________________

Exciting outcomes

1. ______________________________

2. ______________________________

3. ______________________________

PRINTING AND PRODUCTION

Once your book has gone to the printer, it's almost impossible to make changes. Your to-print date is one of the more firm deadlines in publishing. Hot tip: When you're early in the editorial process with your publisher, and softer, more flexible deadlines are set, make it known as early as possible if you need more time!

Questions

1. ______________________________

2. ______________________________

3. ______________________________

Exciting outcomes

1. ____________________

2. ____________________

3. ____________________

DISTRIBUTION AND MARKETING

Marketing plans usually begin around six months before your publication date, but this is not always possible. Your publisher might put together some marketing plans for you, but I encourage you to contribute to marketing your book in ways that we've talked about throughout this journal.

Questions

1. ____________________

2. ____________________

3. ____________________

Exciting outcomes

1. ____________________

2. ____________________

3. ____________________

LAUNCH AND PROMOTION

Hey, hey, look at you! Time for a little celebration. Your book is out in the world. Now is the time for you to think about what it will be like to be out there talking about your book. How can you show up in all the ways that make you, you?

Questions

1. ______________________________

2. ______________________________

3. ______________________________

Exciting outcomes

1. ______________________________

2. ______________________________

3. ______________________________

PUBLISH *Outside-the-Box Promo Ideas*

Hot tip: If you take away anything from this journal, let it be that you have control over how you show up for yourself as a writer. You do not have to pretend to be someone you're not when promoting your book. Being someone else is a huge contributor to burnout, so the more you can get to know who you are, and I mean who you are right now, the better your experience will be and the more energy you will have.

Here's a fun list of some ways you can show up and let people know about your book. Before diving into any of them, make sure they align with who you are, your goals and intentions for your book, and your writerly non-negotiables.

- Be helpful to your fellow authors by sharing more than just your book, and create content based on how you want to show up. I recently made an Instagram Carousel post outlining how I was empowering myself by only saying yes to invites that aligned with the conversations I wanted to be having. There were a lot of comments from other writers who found it helpful!
- Schedule an Instagram Live (or platform of your choice) with someone who has endorsed your book. Ask them questions about how they connected to your book and how it affected them. Your potential readers will want to pick up a copy!
- Create and facilitate a free "how I wrote it" workshop. Folks love hearing about other writers' processes. Or you can create workshops or talks based on the themes in your book. I've created three of these for *Let It Go*. Fun fact: I'm building a course for authors based on this journal.
- Create postcards of your book cover and hand them out like you would business cards. Ask your family and friends to hand them out, too!

- Think about what holidays or important events in the year align with your publication date. How can you tie them to your book? For example, the structure for my fourth book, *Let It Go*, was organized according to the seasons, so I created a follow-along-with-each-season-of-my-book social media strategy, where I took specific topics from that season of my book and posed questions to my audience. This is a great way to build trust with your readers and make them feel included in your process.

- Collaborate with another author to get the word out. Get creative! For example, I reached out to an author who had endorsed my book—and someone I felt I had a genuine connection with—called on my superpower (deep listening through one-on-one intimate conversations), and planned an event with him that highlighted both of our books and our superpowers. Hello, energy increase!

- Use your superpower/specific skill set to showcase the other sides of who you are. I might be doing a live cooking segment on Instagram!

- Do a workshop/live session on the most difficult parts of writing your book. Make sure you revisit **Your Definition of Safety** from the **Prepare** chapter (page 153) before attempting this one.

- Does your book touch on themes that might be relevant for a conference? What gap in their agenda do you see and how can you be the one to fill it? Remember, this is an outside-the-box list, so I'm not talking about writing conferences. Find aligned conferences based on the themes from your book and the conversations you want to be having, and the types of people you want to get in front of. For example, I'm pitching myself to international wellness and mindfulness conferences. I've also landed a speaking gig with a PR firm to talk about slowing down in a fast-paced world. Yes, that's right, I strategically pitched an idea that made sense for how I want to show up and how I can get the word out about my books.

- Call in your personal communities! Are you part of any groups, clubs, or programs filled with people who would want to support you? Tell them about your book. Fun fact: Many of the apps I use for my processes have mini communities where other people who use the apps can connect and share ideas. You better believe I show up and talk about my books there, too!

Add your own ideas to this list. You can also ask your writer peers for suggestions. But only follow through with the activities that make sense for you. Fun fact: The more you allow yourself to show up as your best self, the more possibilities will begin to present themselves! I'm leaning into a speaking career, but instead of saying yes to every invitation and to topics others want me to speak about, I'm building on my own themes and topics that align with who I am and what my message is. Funny how my confidence is starting to show up! The way I show up publicly is finally coming into alignment, and this means I can inspire those who show up to hear me speak. When you're in your element, you will shine.

____

____

____

____

____

____

3 TIPS *For Letting Go of the Glitz*

As a society, we've done a good job of keeping alive the clichéd image of the writer. In movies, we see them gallivanting at high-brow black-tie book launches, schmoozing with publishers at galas, and making a living *only* from their books. For the majority of writers this is *not* anywhere near reality, so when we enter the writing world, we feel misled, unprepared, and, I'll be honest, set up to fail.

Early in my career, I was grateful, honoured, and excited to be selected for a new and very prestigious literary program where the winning writers were offered a stay in a glitzy downtown hotel, a fancy brunch at a fine restaurant, and an elite dinner with a few of the country's top writers. This was the picture I held on to in my head. Oh, *this* is what being an author is like! Wrong. As an industry, we have to do better at helping authors build realistic maps of what it looks like to be a working writer. We have to show them that it's okay not to make all your income directly from writing because there are so many other ways that having a book in the world can bring in exciting and energizing activities that pay your bills. We have to set each other up to live our most authentic creative lives. We have to empower authors to explore all the intricate and intrinsic parts of themselves and build the creative careers that make sense for them as individuals. But whose job is this?

It's rare in publishing to talk about how emotionally taxing promoting a book can be. And when we *do* talk about it, we are reactive rather than proactive, meaning we can easily recognize when folks seem to be out of alignment when promoting their books, or just plain tired, and we provide resources after the fact, instead of setting that author up for success beforehand.

But all hope is not lost! Here are three tips to help you create realistic plans for promoting your book while simultaneously managing your energy. Before using these tips, remember to use your **Say No with Love Map** (page 129) and **Your Book Non-Negotiables** (page 132) from the **Create** chapter to guide your decision-making. Are these promotional activities in alignment with how you want to show up, the conversations you want to be having, and the priorities you are protecting right now? Is this the right time?

1. **Protect your time.** When accepting event invites, tack on an extra hour before and after the event for preparation, debriefs, and reflections. This will allow you to protect the time and space to prepare beforehand and then refill your cup post event. If you cannot include this time, can you still say yes to the event?

    - Get clear about what is expected of you timewise. Are there tech checks you need to take part in? Do you have to attend a social gathering/networking component? I'll never forget the time I said yes to a speaking gig where I was asked to prepare a forty-five-minute talk for an out-of-town conference. I wasn't aware that after my talk I was expected to stay for the full eight-hour conference (with jet-lag in tow)! I couldn't say no with love in the moment because I didn't have these tools at the time. Lesson learned!

2. **Explore your personal definitions of your book promotion success.** Your promotion success shouldn't be defined by the number of events, award galas, or fancy dinners you attend. Remember what's important to you when it comes to your writing and use that as a marker of your self-defined success. Check on that definition you worked on in the **Dream** chapter (page 26).

    Ask yourself: What does success look like for this book? Or what does success look like for you as a writer right now in this moment? Focusing on the present moment can help you pay attention to where you are instead of skipping forward.

3. **Remember that self-promotion is work.** Self-promotion is part of the job of being a writer. It's okay to make people sick of you. It can feel uncomfortable, but imagine a new restaurant owner who never put themselves out there. Find ways to promote yourself while at the same time using your unique superpower. Is there another writer you can include in your social media posts or events? This kind of community call-in is a great way to share the love, build up your circle, and take some of the pressure off yourself.
    - Curate the experience that makes sense for you. You don't have to do what your peers are doing!

WRITING PROMPT *Personal Growing Pains*

In a world where personal growth is a wild adventure, your main character sets out on an extraordinary journey of self-discovery. They'll face unexpected twists and turns, bump into quirky characters, and encounter life lessons that can only be found off the beaten path. Tell the story of their growth, challenges, and amazing transformations that they undergo as they strive to become the most authentic version of themselves.

EXERCISE *Write Your Fears and then Quiet Them*

One of the best things I did for myself early in the promotion of book four was acknowledge what I was afraid of. We can never fully get rid of fear, but we can quiet it when we can predict when and how it will show up. Consider what scares you about your book being in the world and explore three to five ways you might quiet those fears. Revisit your **Safe** (page 10) and your **Inventory** (page 12). Think about your circle. You are not alone!

Chelene's Vault

One of my writerly fears was that people wouldn't understand why I jump from genre to genre. I went from poetry to memoir to fiction to narrative nonfiction to guided journals! I saw this variety as a flaw until a good friend (she's a writer, too) reminded me that writers are multi-layered artists. After our conversation, and a beautiful mindful walk around a lake, I realized that exploring different genres is a part of who I am. I made a list of all the writers I admire who also write in multiple genres. What I have to say can't always fit into the same container. I looked at the connecting themes in my books and saw a thread of love, care, and support, no matter the genre. Let's just say I kicked that fear to the curb because I slowed down long enough to acknowledge it was there.

Reflection

Be Kind, but Be Honest

A consistent reflection practice will allow you to track your personal growth, because when you look back at your reflections you will be able to pinpoint what's changed and what you've learned. Spend a few minutes reflecting on how you feel about the materials you worked through in the **Publish** chapter. What surprises you? What excites you? What scares you? Write like no one will ever read this.

CHECK-IN CORNER *Let Go and Keep Safe*

Did anything surprise you in the **Publish** chapter? You can drop it off in the **Mind Dump** (page 15). Is there anything you need to add to your **Inventory** (page 12) or **Safe** (page 10)?

Part 3

After Publishing

Everything I see or do, the weather and the water, buildings... everything actual is an advantage when I am writing. It is like a menu, or a giant tool box, and I can pick and choose what I want.
—Toni Morrison

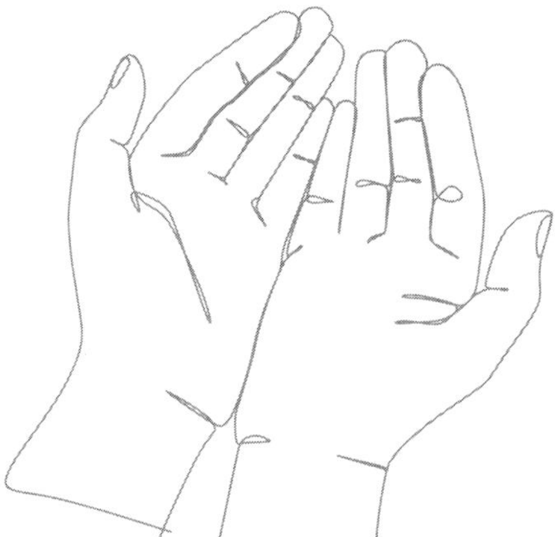

Chapter 8

Keep Safe

It's time to revisit the Safe and learn how to protect your book experiences.

KEEP SAFE *Intention and Affirmation*

My intention for this chapter is to

The affirmation I will say to myself throughout this chapter to hold up that intention is

KEEP SAFE *Revisit the Safe*

Writing a book is worthy of celebration whether you publish it or not. And publishing a book is also a big deal! It's celebratory *and* it's scary. But even though you don't have control over the outcome, you do have control over how you show up. With each book experience, you will notice the journey becoming more and more intentional and closer to what you envision for your creative life.

Before you move through the final section of this journal, go back. Looking back and engaging in a regular reflection practice is one of the best ways to track your growth and evolution as a writer. Look closely at how your mindset has shifted, how you've let go of old narratives, and how you've curated a unique journey for you and your book. Look at what you've experienced and be in awe of yourself. I know how mindset shifts and reflective work can transform a person's outlook and motivation. We can't expect others to celebrate us with love and light if we aren't willing to do it for ourselves.

Are you ready?

As you near the end of this book journey, no matter where you started in the journal, you should have some things of value tucked away in the **Safe** (page 10). Now is your opportunity to revisit the **Safe** and celebrate all the things you want to protect moving forward. Spend time with each item in your **Safe** and write a few lines about why you wanted to keep this item safe and what it might mean for you and your *next* book.

If this guided writing doesn't feel accessible to you, that's okay; instead, try writing about what you want to do with the items in your **Safe**.

Chelene's Vault

My idea for this guided journal started at the end of promoting my second book. I'd scribble my ideas, experiences, and dreams in a notebook. I used my notebook to reflect after difficult events, and I wrote in the notebook to celebrate after wonderful events. The notebook made me feel safe and, as a writer, unstoppable. Knowing that my journal was always with me made me feel powerful. When it came time to promote my third and fourth books, I felt like I could show up and be present in the moment because I wasn't worried about time moving too fast, and I wasn't trying to hold everything in my head. Everything I needed and wanted to hold on to was in my journal. It was...safe. I wish I'd had the idea for the journal earlier, but it's never too late to give the rest of the world the tools I had always wanted for myself. There's something beautiful about that.

KEEP SAFE *Protect Your Non-Negotiables*

It is so important for writers to prioritize their non-negotiables by building an emotional narrative around them. Writers often miss this step, which is why we find ourselves saying yes to situations, opportunities, and editorial suggestions that do not align with our goals, values, and intentions. To feel confident moving forward, you absolutely must build your emotional narratives around the things you want to protect and prioritize. So let's flex those muscles now.

Look back at the non-negotiables you wrote in the **Create** chapter (page 135) and select three to build an emotional narrative around to make them stick. Remember, you've already had some practice writing emotional narratives in the **Dream** (page 29) and **Learn** (pages 65–66) chapters. You can do this for all your book's non-negotiables, but let's start with three.

____

____

____

Imagine you're living in a world where honouring these non-negotiables is an impossible feat. Imagine what it would feel like to have to toss these non-negotiables away and to know they were completely off the table. What would this mean for you and your book? Brainstorm on the next page.

Now, imagine that these non-negotiables were honoured. What would your experience be like then?

Sit inside both versions and allow yourself to move forward in life protecting these non-negotiables because you can see the emotional weight of not having them, but you can also feel what it would be like to have protected them. Let these feelings be the emotional narrative you lean on.

After such a deep exercise, you may need to let something go. Do you need to visit the **Mind Dump** (page 15)? While you're there, consider looking over all the beliefs, ideas, narratives, and learnings you've dropped off so far. Be proud! These no longer serve you and they don't have to take up space in your head anymore.

3 TIPS *For Valuing Your Work*

We live in a time when we know the cost of everything, but we tend to forget what things are worth. What price would you put on your joy? Try these three tips for valuing your writing projects:

1. **Create a metaphor for how writing plays a role in your life.** Once you have your metaphor, bring it up in conversation as much as you can. When you're speaking about your book in public, or even having coffee with friends, build a narrative around how important your writing practice is. You can make your metaphor as simple or as complex as you like.

For example: *To me, writing is water. I can only go so long without it.*

Build an emotional narrative around your metaphor for writing and watch how you start to protect your work and your experience. Bonus: The people around you will start to understand that writing is a part of who you are.

____

____

____

____

____

2. **Place a monetary value on the *outcome* of your book being in the world instead of just the book itself.** Book advances don't define who we are (see page 158). Writers need to be

a lot more savvy about how we make money from our books. Pull from the **Entrepreneurial Writer** section in the **Prepare** chapter (page 158) and further outline the types of speaking gigs, workshops, and other paid opportunities you can build around your book. You can make a living as a writer if you embrace writing-adjacent work and think about growing your creative career based on who you are, how you want to show up, and what gives you energy. Heck, this might even help you plan future book ideas.

Bonus: This tip connects to growing your author brand, and it's often the author's brand that helps sell the book.

3. **Extract the top three themes from your book and brainstorm ways to monetize them.** For example, I turned my last book's theme of letting go of old beliefs into a paid keynote and a mini workshop. And I'm building this journal into my coaching program. Next, revisit **Your Circle** from the **Prepare** chapter (page 155). Who can help you get the word out about your new offerings?

1. ______________________________

____

2. ______________________________

____

3. ______________________________

____

Chelene's Vault

All the suggestions and methods in this journal are techniques I've personally experimented with. I transformed a modest four-figure advance into a substantial salary by making decisions that made sense for me. There were people in my life who didn't fully believe in me. When I squint my eyes, I still see them today. Their words "Oh, okay, but when this doesn't work out ..." are still undulating in my head, but they hold no value today. My ability to read people meant I could tell that they assumed I was making mistakes when I let go of paying gigs (that didn't align) or insider roles in publishing (where I couldn't show up as my best self), but I knew I was being strategic. I was being intentional. I was putting myself first. I could see ten steps ahead because I built the lenses I was looking through. Was it a walk in the park? Far from it. Yet, because every step I take aligns strategically with my identity and goals, decision-making demands far less energy than before. Taking bold leaps, like pitching myself and my offerings, feels less daunting because it's rooted in a purposeful direction. But it all started with dreaming. I hope you can dream yourself here, too.

WRITING PROMPT *What Will You Change?*

How will you take your book journey deeper? When we think about what we have control over in our writerly journey, letting go of the aspects that no longer serve us is a big one. Look back over your **Reflections** in the journal. What can you drop off in the **Mind Dump** (page 15) one last time? In the space below, share your thoughts on what you want to change for your next book.

EXERCISE *Plan Your Next Project*

Congrats for making it to the end of this journal! It must feel pretty darn good to now have a complete keepsake of your book journey. Maybe your next project has already been in the works for some time. Maybe your previous book sparked an idea for the next one. Celebrate here! Take a moment to express gratitude for every experience. It all counts. It all informs the writer you're becoming. You may or may not already have a good idea of what your next book project will be about; either way, put some thoughts down here.

What worked well with my last project? How can I call more of this in?

What is my new book idea?

What excites me about this new book idea?

What scares me about the new book idea, and how can I lean into that fear in a safe way?

What will I do to make sure I call in more joy with the next book?

How have I grown as a person?

Reflection

Be Kind, but Be Honest

Completing this journal means you've got a genuine record of your writing journey. No matter what comes next with your book project, you'll always have this keepsake. I hope it has given you clarity about where you belong in the writing world—the next steps are entirely your call. Writing can be hard work, and for some, it turns into a business. But without joy, what's the point? Remember, even though there are many aspects of your writing journey that may be out of your hands and moments that take a bit too much energy from you, you have full control over how you show up.

Don't forget to keep a fresh journal for each book you're working on. These journals become invaluable keepsakes, encapsulating your journey as a writer. Whether you plan to publish your work or not, they can be incredibly useful for troubleshooting and improving your writing process. You are a writer.

Spend a few minutes reflecting on how you feel about the materials you worked through in the **Keep Safe** chapter. What surprised you? What excites you? What scares you? Revisit the **Inventory** (page 12) one last time. How do you feel?

Acknowledgements

I'm overflowing with love and gratitude for the amazing folks in my life who've had my back over the years, cheering on my big ideas and outside-the-box thinking. Seriously, I wouldn't be where I am in my career without you all.

Huge shoutout to the writers who've trusted me with their stories over the years. Your faith in me means the world. And to my home team, Oliver and Richard—you've seen me through the ups and downs, the rejections, the mess-ups, and the moments of self-discovery. You're the real MVPS.

Big love to my agent, Sam Haywood, for always having my back. And a massive thanks to everyone at House of Anansi, especially my editor, Shirarose Wilensky—the queen of line edits, no doubt!

This time, I gotta give a special shoutout to everyone in the Forever Writers Club. Your support and early love for this project kept me going. You all rock!

To everyone who's been a part of this journey, thank you from the bottom of my heart.

Maxine Bulloch

About the Author

Chelene Knight is the author of five books, including *Let It Go: Free Yourself from Old Beliefs and Find a New Path to Joy*. Chelene is a certified mindfulness facilitator and creative balance coach. Over the past decade, Chelene has meticulously cultivated a robust portfolio of workshops and custom support for authors and busy professionals. Her unwavering commitment to nurturing community has birthed an empathetic editorial approach and a mentorship-driven ethos that aids emerging writers in their development. Chelene was the previous managing editor at *Room* magazine, festival director for the Growing Room Festival in Vancouver, and worked as a literary agent with the Transatlantic Agency. She has also worked as a professor of poetry at the University of Toronto and the University of British Columbia. She is founder of the Forever Writers Club, a membership for writers focused on creative balance, and is founder of her own creative studio, Breathing Space Creative, through which she's launched the Thrive Coaching Program, where busy creatives can learn how to manage their energy and make space for all the things they are passionate about.

Did you enjoy peeking into Chelene's vault? Continue the journey. Sign up for a Chelene's Vault subscription at cheleneknight.com and learn more about her other resources for writers.

About Breathing Space Creative

Breathing Space's vision is to empower professional creative go-getters to reclaim their time for self-care and pursue their dreams while achieving a joyful work-life balance. Through the Thrive Coaching Program, using the Say No with Love Method, Breathing Space Creative wholeheartedly supports professionals and creative entrepreneurs in defining and confidently advocating for their boundaries, while nurturing their passions. We deeply cherish the wisdom gained from personal journeys, acknowledging that every story holds invaluable expertise. Additionally, we are committed to shedding outdated narratives that burden us. Our ultimate goal is to facilitate growth, evolution, release, and self-discovery.

Transformation commences when we transform our perceptions of various life aspects, including the self. This transformation journey begins by delving into the root causes of our challenges, examining our thought patterns, belief systems, environments, and information absorption methods. Self-reflection stands as the cornerstone of this transformative process.

breathingspacecreative.com